HISTORY OF SARGENT COUNTY
VOLUME 2 – 1880-1920
FORMAN-GWINNER-MILNOR & SARGENT COUNTY VETERANS

By Susan Mary Kudelka

HISTORY OF SARGENT COUNTY
VOLUME 2 - 1880-1920
FORMAN-GWINNER-MILNOR & SARGENT COUNTY VETERANS

Copyright © 2004 by Susan Mary Kudelka

All rights reserved.

No part of this book may be reproduced or transmitted in any form or by any means electronic or mechanical, including photocopying, recording, or by any information storage and retrieval system, without permission in writing from the copyright owner.

Author - Susan Mary Kudelka
Publisher - McCleery & Sons Publishing

NOTE: The maps shown are from the 1909 Sargent County Standard Atlas.

International Standard Book Number: 1-931916-35-7

Printed in the United States of America

FUTURE BOOKS

*Future books will include The Great Depression,
World War II, ghost towns in Sargent County,
town histories, business histories and much more.*

I dedicate this book to my Uncle Dennis Eugene Kudelka. Growing up on a farm in Sargent County, Dennis was extremely familiar with the area. As a young man, he was very inquisitive, he always wanted to know how things worked. At age fifteen, he disassembled his parents Victrola to see for himself how it worked. He used this interest to become a successful auto mechanic. It was never too cold for Dennis to work on a car. After high school, he attended and graduated from North Dakota State College of Science and was soon drafted into the U.S. Army. He served for two years in the motor pool and was stationed in Thailand. Soon afterwards he married Sharon Heath. Dennis worked as a Ford Certified Auto Mechanic at Berube's in Lisbon, North Dakota. In his spare time, he enjoyed hunting, fishing, camping and exploring Ransom and Sargent Counties. Dennis passed away on April 30th, 2003.

TABLE OF CONTENTS

Chapter 1
Early History of Sargent County 1

Chapter 2
World War I Veterans from Sargent County 7

Chapter 3
Civil War Veterans 72

Chapter 4
Sargent County Fair 74

Chapter 5
Forman 78

Chapter 6
Gwinner 133

Chapter 7
Milnor 159

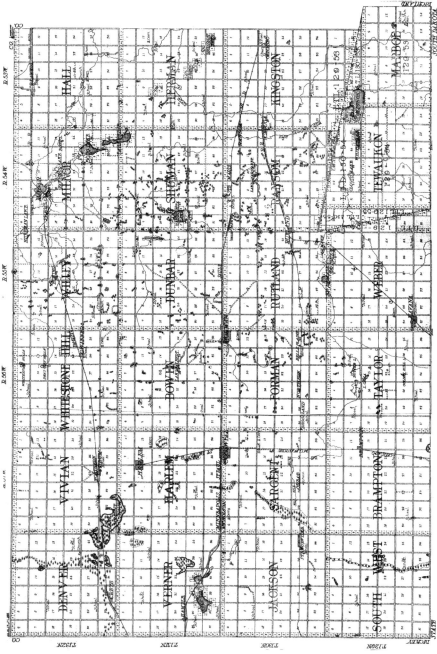

CHAPTER 1

Early History of Sargent County
Written by H. A. Soule in 1924

Hiram Allen Soule was born in North Fairfax, Vermont on March 30th, 1853. When Hiram was ten years old he and his family moved to Ripon, Wisconsin. He lived there until the spring of 1874 when he went to Yankton, South Dakota, then the capital of Dakota Territory. Mr. Soule applied for work with Mr. E. H. Van Antwerp, United States Deputy Surveyor. He secured the job because he was the only one who could read a compass besides Mr. Antwerp.[1] By 1877, he was a United States Deputy Surveyor. A few years later, in 1890, he was U.S. Surveyor for Sargent, Sheridan and Bowman Counties. He was Sargent County Surveyor for forty years.[2] The following is his story of surveying in Sargent County.

In the spring of 1879, Mr. W. H. Antwerp received a contract from the government to survey a number of townships that were situated along the extreme south side of what is now known as Ransom County. We left Yankton, South Dakota in the latter part of May. Mr. Antwerp left on the train and I was to take the outfit overland and meet him at Lake Kampeski, now Watertown. We went up the James River to about where Huron, South Dakota now stands, then we went a north easterly direction to Lake Kampeski, which had been for some time the terminus of the old Winona and St. Peters Railroad. This road has been built some years before but was little used. I think they ran a train over it but once a week. The end of the road was the lake. Watertown was about two miles east. It started that spring and was a very small village containing about forty or fifty inhabitants. Here we met Mr. Antwerp.

There was an old military trail that left the lake and ran north to Fort Wadsworth. About two years after this time the name of this fort was changed to Fort Sisseton. The trail ran close to a large lone

2   *Susan Mary Kudelka*

tree, that was the extreme southern point of the Sisseton Indian Reservation, which is wedge, shaped with a sharp point to the south.

We soon found rougher country and between the hills were many lakes. We were now in the coteaus, so named by the early French explorers meaning hills. The trail led us between many of these lakes and became so split up that it was extremely hard to follow and we soon lost it and got tangled up in so many lakes and sloughs that we thought we never would get out.

We finally found a place where some one had been cutting cord wood and from there a road leading north which we followed and about sundown drove into Fort Wadsworth. I think there were companies of soldiers stationed there at that time and it was large enough to accommodate many more. It was here that Yellowstone Kelly, the noted scout and guide, first struck Dakota. He came at the close of the Civil War and afterwards helped build Fort Ransom on the Sheyenne River, where he was discharged. The next morning, we left Fort Wadsworth on the old military trail that led to Fort Ransom. This road was well defined. It had been made by large military wagons that were wider than common ones and had in former years been much used, as over this trail were hauled supplies to Fort Ransom, Fort Sewart and Fort Totten. On every high point of the road large mounds were thrown up for guides. At about five o'clock we crossed the Seventh Standard Parallel, which is now the line that divides North and South Dakota.

At that time there we no white settlers in what is now Sargent County. There was a half-breed by the name of John Longie who had a log house on the west end of Lake Tewaukon. After crossing the Seventh Parallel we soon began to descend the coteaus and passed down the ridge just west of the gulch where Dan Lynch used to live and reached the level prairies. Passing over level prairies we soon came to a lake and as it was near night we decided to camp and after setting up our tents we went to the lake for water. After wading out for several rods we could only find about an inch of water so we had to dig a well on the shore to get enough water for camp use.

This is now called Sprague's Lake, so named for the first settler in the east end. The next morning we did not drive more than a

History of Sargent County - Vol. 2 - 1880-1920

quarter of a mile when we came to a smaller lake with good deep water now called Silver Lake. We passed to the east of this and soon passed a little east of where Pete Narum now lives, then north and a little west; we must have passed close to where the Rutland Consolidated School now stands. John Nockleby's house, which is just two miles east of Forman, stands on the old trail.

In the spring of 1881, General W. H. H. Beadle received a contract to survey what is now Hall and Herman Townships. Upon inquiring we were informed that a man by the name of Ezra Post lived on the land where we were to survey. We managed to get over almost impassable roads and reached Mr. Post, who lived in the extreme eastern part of what is now Sargent County on the Wild Rice River in the first grove in the sand hills along the river. Mr. Ezra Post and family, Mr. Hiram Harrington and family, Mr. Jas. Davis and Mr. Frank Strong came here to what is called Hamlin. June 20th, 1879, Mr. Harrington built his house of logs. His was the first white man's house in Sargent County. Mr. Post hauled lumber from Wahpeton for his house. Mr. Davis went back east and moved his family out here in the summer of 1880. Mr. John Goolsby and John Herman came in 1880. Mr. Daniel Thornton and family also came this spring.

On the third day of July a stranger appeared in the camp and invited us to a Fourth of July celebration that was to be held in Jim Davis' grove the next day. We went to the celebration, which was certainly the first Fourth of July celebration held in Sargent County. There was a big feed and a dance both which every one enjoyed.

In the spring of 1882, we started work in Milnor Township and worked westward through what is now Willey Township and then through Whitestone Hill and Vivian Township. In Milnor Township we found many shacks belonging to people who had come to take up claims. All these settlers were there as squatters and made claims upon un-surveyed land. If the settler didn't happen to be home we could usually find his name written somewhere on his shack and could thereby attach his name to the land surveyed. In some cases a shack was found but no person or no name. We found it difficult to make out our full report of surveyed land with its owner's name. There was usually a piece of breaking on the land near the shack. We

4 *Susan Mary Kudelka*

were instructed by the Department of Interior to take note of this and all other improvements on all land. Many of the shacks were made with sod walls and perhaps lumber roof and door. They seemed hardly habitable and were put up usually as a sign of claim that had been made. However, some of these shacks were made into homes as the greater part of the early settlers were young people who felt they could put up with a great deal if they could only clinch the land. The shacks ranged in size from eight by eight feet to twelve by fourteen feet. The latter size was usual. Willey Township named after a man by the name of A. B. Willey with whom we became quite well acquainted in after years.

We ran across some hills in what is now called Whitestone Hill Township. These hills were erroneously named, supposing that these hills were the White Stone Hills of Sully's battlefield. We found traces of a camping ground and upon investigation found a spring. The old military road had followed Indian trails to this spring. It was very hard to get water on the prairie and the whites usually followed Indian trails that frequently led to springs.

Back in 1862, over this Indian trail leading to this spring before the trail was made a military road there passed a band of Indians under a chief named White Lodge, who was carrying away from a settlement on Shetak Lake in southwestern Minnesota, two white women, Mrs. Wright and Mrs. Daly and seven white children. This band passed up to Big Stone Lake on to Skunk Lake and up through Sargent County over the old Indian trail that led to Whitestone Hill springs then on up to where Fort Ransom was afterwards built on the bluff of the Sheyenne River, then on to the northwest to the headwaters of Bear Creek. They had drifted over to the Missouri River to the mouth of Beaver creek where they were discovered by Major C. E. Golpin, who, when reaching Fort Pierre informed a band of mixed blood Indians under the leadership of Martin Charger, grandson of Captain Lewis of the Lewis and Clark expedition, that he had seen the captives here. Martin Charger and his band were successful in freeing these women and children and sent them home to southern Minnesota.

In Whitestone Hill and Bowen Townships, I found O. F. Johnson,

Nils Petterson, I. G. Carlblom, J. F. Carlblom, C. O. Johnson, Jels P. Lund, Erick Backlund, John Swanson, Nels Bjork, Magnus Bjork, A. G. Anderson, Erick Anderson, Oluf Melroe, L. E. Halin, Hans Severson and A. E. Stevens. Later we moved our outfit to Vivian Township where we became acquainted with Messers, Smith, Barton and Stewart. In the southwest part of Vivian Township there is a slough now known as the Crete Slough. Around this slough there were some trees growing which were the only scattering trees in Sargent County except in the eastern part on the Wild Rice River.

From here we passed south into Harlem Township. The only men with whom I remember coming in contact with was Homer Mills, his brother Simeon and a brother of A. M. Cook. From there we went into Bowen Township. After reaching about the center we met Mr. Ed Bowen after whom the township was named. Mr. Bowen informed us that it would be useless to survey east in Bowen because the country was so stony that it would never be settled. Within a year, the township was settled and every quarter was filed on.

From Bowen we went into Kingston Township. While in Kingston there was more standing water in Sargent County than has ever been since, except in the summer of 1916. This made it extremely hard to survey because we found it difficult to distinguish between a lake and a slough. We met John Devlin, Austin Cryan and his brothers, Michael and Joseph, two King brothers and Mr. W. E. Dada, whom I believe lived just across in Ransom.

From there we went west into Ransom Township where we ran across Randolph Holding living where the town of Ransom now stands. We moved on to Rutland Township. In this township we were camped about two miles from where Rutland now stands. We moved into Forman Township where we found the low places filled with water. As usual this situation made surveying very difficult. John Miller and many others had claims in this township.

We entered Sargent Township at the northeast corner of Section 24 where W. W. Lamb now lives. We drove two miles west and camped in what is now Mr. Pieper's pasture. In this township we became acquainted with Geo. S. Montgomery and Pat. Rourke. These men later started a village called Blackstone, which was later called

Sargent. I recall that Richard McCarten, Henry McCarten, John McGraw and Frank McGraw, O. B. Blanchard and many more had laid claim to land around here. Some of these men we did not see, but obtained their names from their shanty doors and recorded their names along with a description of the land in our field notes.

Just across in Brampton Township we found Henry Ashley's shanty. We also found Oka Ashley's not far from his fathers. When we were surveying the line between Sections 1 and 2, little did I thought that in four years a railroad would be running right over this line and that in 1890 a village would spring up here at the junction of the Milwaukee and St. Paul and the Soo Line Railroads, that would eventually be named Cogswell, nor did I foresee that eleven years later I would move here and live until the present date.

---

[1] H. A. Soule information, written by Lucretia Soule.
[2] S.M. Thorfinnson, *Sargent County History* (Sargent County Commissioners publishers, 1976), 152.

CHAPTER 2
World War I Veterans from Sargent County

The United States officially entered World War I on April 6th, 1917 by declaring war on Germany. Shortly after entering the war, Congress enacted the Selective Service Act of May 1917. It required all males between the ages of eighteen to forty-five. "The result was the registration of over ten million young men, of whom the Army eventually drafted 2.7 million."[1] The following is a list of men from Sargent County that participated in World War I.

"**John Gotfreid Anderson** of Milnor, born in Sweden in 1891, entered service March 29th, 1918, trained at Camp Dodge, Iowa and Camp Mills, New York; started over-seas May 20th, 1918, was engaged in the battle of St. Mihiel, Argonne, Belleau and the Marne, was killed December 11th, 1918, by the accidental discharge of a revolver."

"**Charles Andrew Collier** of Cogswell, born in Clear Lake, Iowa, September 25th, 1893, entered service July 23rd, 1917, trained at Camp Greene, North Carolina, two months and Camp Mills, New York, one month; started over-seas December 12th, 1917, served in Company "M" 18th Infantry, under General Bullard; was engaged in battle of Cantigny and second Battle of Marne. Shell wound in left knee on morning of July 18th, 1918, at beginning of the big drive, resulting in amputation of left leg above knee. Discharged February 19th, 1919."

"**Sergeant Leo E. Brooks** of Cogswell, born at St. Cloud, Minnesota, March 23rd, 1896; entered service April 7th, 1917, trained at Jefferson Barracks, Mo., six months; Kelly Field, Texas, nineteen months and at Sam Houston, San Antonio, Texas."

"**Lynn Ferdinand Johnson** of Havana, born at Havana, November 8th, 1896; entered service November 5th, 1918; trained at the Agriculture College, North Dakota, from November 5th, 1918 to December 9th, 1918, when discharged."

"**Will H. Rehborg** of Gwinner, born in Iowa, December 24th, 1893; entered service June 24th, 1918; trained at Camp Dodge six weeks and started overseas; served in the 88th Division, Company 352."

John Gotfreid Anderson, Charles Andrew Collier, Sergeant Leo E. Brooks, Lynn Ferdinand Johnson, Will H. Rehborg

Arthur Nelson, Lars Hillestad, John William Gallus, Olaf Romstad, Edward Gilbertson

"**Arthur Nelson** of Roslyn, South Dakota, born at Minneapolis, Minnesota, May 26th, 1892; entered service September 1st, 1918; trained at Grand Forks, North Dakota, two months and Camp Shelby, Mississippi, two months. Discharged December 21st, 1918."

"**Lars Hillestad** of Rutland, born in Bellingham, Minnesota, February 1st, 1894; entered service July 22nd, 1918 trained at Camp Custer seven months and Camp Dodge six days; served in 14th Division, Company "D", 78th Infantry under Captain J. D. Convill; discharged February 7th, 1919."

"**John William Gallus** of Geneseo, born in Arcadin, Wisconsin, March 6th, 1897; entered service September 5th, 1917; trained at Camp Grant two months and in Camp McArthur, two months and Camp Dodge ten days; served in Company "G" 2nd Battalion, under Lieutenant Inglbritson; discharged January 10th, 1919."

"**Olaf Romstad** of Oakes born in Sargent County, August 18th, 1897; entered service March 1st, 1918; trained at Jefferson Barracks one month, Kelly Field one month, Wilbur Wright Field two months; started over-seas June 22nd, 1918, served in 95th Aero Squadron of 15th Present Group, under commanding officer, Alfred M. Joyce; was engaged in battle of Argonne and St. Mihiel; discharged March 22nd, 1919."

"**Edward Gilbertson** of Cogswell, born September 6th, 1893; entered service September, 1918; trained at Camp Dodge two months and at Camp Pike six and one-half months; started overseas June 20th, served in the 2nd Division, Company "C" 9th Infantry, under Captain Arthur A. Harrington; was engaged in Belleau Wood battle, St. Mihiel and Sedan."

Corporal Magnus Peter Romstad, Captain Edwin Arthur Goltz, Thomas N. McFarland, Sergeant Hilding Einar Safstrom, Neely Clyde Bierce

"**Corporal Magnus Peter Romstad** of Oakes, born in Sargent County, September 6th, 1892; entered service at Northfield, Iowa, about five months; started overseas in July 1918; served in the 88th Division 351st Infantry Band, Headquarters Company

"**Captain Edwin Arthur Goltz** of Havana, born in Wahpeton, North Dakota, May 11th, 1892; entered service April 29th, 1918; trained at Camp Dodge, Iowa, three and one-half months; started overseas August 8th, 1918; served in the 88th Division, Company "B."

"**Thomas N. McFarland** of Gwinner, born in Sargent County, August 24th, 1894; entered service July 22nd, 1918; trained at Camp Custer, Michigan, six months, fourteen days and Camp Dodge six days, served in Division 14, Company "H," 78th Infantry, under Captain Kerr and Captain Rockwood, discharged February 11th, 1919."

"**Sergeant Hilding Einar Safstrom** of Staples, Minnesota, born in Rullbo, Sweden, October 24th, 1891; entered service September 21st, 1917; trained at Camp Dodge, Iowa, ten months, started over-seas August 3rd, 1918, served in the 88th Division, H. Q. Company, 352nd Infantry, under Major General Weigel; was engaged twenty-one days on Haute Alsace Front; discharged March 25th, 1919."

"**Neely Clyde Bierce** of Havana, born in Iola, Wisconsin, July 29th, 1892; entered service in March 1914; trained eight months at United States Naval Training Station, Great Lakes, Illinois and one week on training ship at Boston, Massachusetts. Then assigned as Chief Quartermaster U. S. S. Des Moines, New York, N.Y. Made over twenty round trips in guarding transports during war."

"**Hjalmer Rolie** of Havana, born in Hankinson, North Dakota, June 23rd, 1898; entered service April 18th, 1917; trained at Camp Cody nine months, started over-seas in June 1918; served in 36th Division, 1st Quartermaster, 414 Motor Supply Train, 438 Motor Truck Company."

"**Austin Francis Bierce** of Havana, born in Iola, Wisconsin, March 31st, 1900; entered service in April 1918; trained at Great Lakes, then to Training Ship U.S.S. Hartford, at Navy Yard, Charleston, South Carolina; served under the command of Lieutenant Nightingale."

"**Basil Lloyd Bierce** of Owatonna, Minnesota, born in Iola, Wisconsin, April 23rd, 1894; entered service in May 1917, trained at Camp Cody from September 1917, to late in August 1918, then to Camp Dix for a few weeks. Started over-seas in September 1918; served originally with Supply Company, 2nd Minnesota, later made part of the 136th Infantry, which was disrupted after reaching Europe; then Sub. Dept. No. 3, A. P. O. 762, A. E. F."

"**Joseph W. Powers** of Havana, born in La Fayette, Wisconsin; entered service July 10th, 1918; trained at Fort Riley, Kansas, three months, Camp Lee, Virginia, six weeks and Camp Mills; started over-seas in November; served in 18th Veb. Hospital Unit."

Hjalmer Rollie, Austin Francis Bierce, Basil Lloyd Bierce, Joseph W. Powers

Alex Leonard Sannes, James Dallas Busey, George Clifton Brooks, Ejnar Erickson, Frank J. Lommel

"**Alex Leonard Sannes** of Forman, born in Forman November 19th, 1891; entered service September 19th, 1917; trained at Camp Dodge two months and Camp Pike seven months; started over-seas June 20th, served in the 26th Division, Company "B," 10th Infantry, under Captain Goodmanson was engaged in the Battle of Chateau Thierry."

"**James Dallas Busey** of Havana, born in Alexandria, Minnesota, June 30th, 1895; entered service March 29th, 1918; trained at Camp Dodge four months; started over-seas August 15th, 1918, served as musician in the 88th Division, Headquarters Company, under General Weizel."

"**George Clifton Brooks** of Geneseo, born in Geneseo, February 24th, 1896; entered service June 30th, 1918; trained at Grand Forks, North Dakota, eight weeks; Fort Leavenworth, Kansas and New York City nearly five months; discharged January 22nd, 1919."

"**Ejnar Eriksen** of Milnor, born in Denmark, June 2nd, 1895; entered service September 19th, 1917, trained at Camp Dodge, Iowa, two and one-half months, Camp Pike, Arkansas seven months, Fort Sam Houston, Texas, six months; discharged January 11th, 1919."

"**Frank J. Lommel** of Havana, born at Farmington, Minnesota, September 28th, 1890; entered service August 31st, 1918; trained at Grand Forks, North Dakota, University two months; Austin, Texas, University, two and one-half months; Camp Funston, Kansas, two weeks. (With Radio Band at Austin, Texas, during entire period while in that camp.) Discharged January 31st, 1919."

Helmer Olive Halvorson, Gustav Lewis Halmrast, William Orville Austin, Ray H. Brooks, Nels Gardner

"**Helmer Oliver Halvorson** of Milnor, born in Richland County, North Dakota, December 2nd, 1897; entered service April 21st, 1917; trained at Great Lakes from April until July, Sault River Camp Neebish. Michigan, until October 18th; Philadelphia until February 15th, 1918, when starting over-seas; served in Northern Bombing Group, Field A, France, U. S. Naval Aviation Forces."

"**Gustav Lewis Halmrast** of DeLamere, born at DeLamere, January 1st, 1897; entered service in April 1918; trained at Jefferson Barracks, Washington Barracks and Camp Merritt; started over-seas in June 1918; served in Company "B," 32nd Division, was engaged in the Battle at Verdun, Meuse and Argonne."

"**William Orville Austin** of Havana, born in Sauk Center, Minnesota, October 29th, 1892; entered service September 19th, 1917; trained at Camp Dodge two months, Camp Pike four months, Camp Greene three weeks and Camp Mills two weeks; started over-seas in May 1918; served in Headquarters Company, 47th Infantry, 4th Division, under Major General Cameron."

"**Ray H. Brooks** of Geneseo, born in Cavalier, North Dakota, August 18th, 1892; entered service June 24th, 1918; trained at Camp Dodge. Iowa, four months and seven and one-half months at Camp Cody, N. Mexico. Served in the 88th Division two months and Development Batt. No. 2 three and one-half months. Discharged December 11th, 1918."

"**Nels Gardner** of Forman, born in Kolbu Toten, Norway, October 10th, 1891; entered service July 20th, 1918; trained at Camp Custer, Michigan eight months, served in the 14th Division, Company "A," 78th Infantry; was discharged March 19th, 1919."

"**John E. Backlin** of Oakes, born in Sargent County, March 18th, 1897; entered service February 22nd, 1918; trained at Ware Island, California and Bay Shore, Long Island, N. Y.; served in Bay Shore Aviator's Station; discharged February 19th, 1919."

"**Samuell Neil Noyes** of Cogswell, born at Beaver Dam, Wisconsin, December 26th, 1894; entered service June 24th, 1918; trained at Camp Dodge, six weeks; started overseas August 16th, 1918; served in 88th Division, 352 Reg. Company "M" Infantry."

"**Oscar D. Rosenwater** of Milnor, born at Milnor, October 1st, 1890; entered service August 25th; trained at Camp Lewis, Washington, Fort Stevens, Camp Austin, Va. and Camp Dodge, Iowa, discharged December 24th, 1918."

"**Ole Jacob Millerhagen** of Forman, born in Norway, March 22nd, 1890; entered service March 29th, 1918; trained at Camp Dodge and Camp Upton, Long Island; started overseas June 1918; served in 39th Engineers' Corps." He remained in the service after the war.

"**Robert W. Safstrom** of Gwinner, born in Sweden, December 5th, 1887; entered service March 29th, 1918; trained at Camp Dodge, Iowa; started overseas May 2nd, 1918; served in Company "M" 138th Infantry, 35th Division; was engaged in the Argonne battle, where wounded by high explosives through left shoulder, the 26th of September, 1918; discharged from service May 12th, 1919."

John E. Backlin, Samuell Neil Noyes, Oscar D. Rosenwater, Ole Jacob Millerhagen, Robert W. Safstrom

"**Raymond Ernest Bauch** of Forman, born at Rutland, March 10th, 1897; entered service April 14th, 1917; started overseas November 3rd, 1917; served at Gibraltar from there to Lisbon, Portugal and Bizerta, Africa; discharged."

"**Sergeant David Hannum Jones** of Forman, born in Rutland, September 19th, 1895; entered service April 29th, 1918; trained at Camp Dodge, Iowa, from date of enlistment until discharged January 27th, 1919."

"**Elvin M. Johnson** of Havana, born at Havana, August 27th, 1891; entered service September 1917; trained at Camp Dodge, two months, Camp Pike, five months, Camp Green, one month and Camp Merritt, one week; started overseas June 1918; served in Company "D" 4th Division, A. T. A. E. F.; was engaged in the battle of Chateau Thierry, St. Mihiel, Argonne and Meuse; discharged August 5th, 1919, at Camp Dodge."

"**Julius B. Abrahamson** of Gwinner, born in Willmar, Minnesota, September 17th, 1892; entered service and trained at Agricultural College, Fargo, North Dakota and Fort Bliss, Texas; served in Motor Transport Corps, under Major Schillo's command; discharged January 21st, 1919."

"**Otto William Olson** of Milnor, born at Milnor, March 28th, 1893; entered service September 5th, 1918; trained at Camp Grant, three weeks and from there to Hancock, Ga.; discharged at Camp Dodge, January 9th, 1919."

Raymond Ernest Bauch, Sergeant David Hannum Jones, Elvin M. Johnson, Julius B. Abrahamson, Otto William Olson

"**John Edward Davis** of Forman, born in Arcadia, Wisconsin, January 13th, 1891; entered service March 29th, 1918; trained at Camp Dodge one month and Camp Mills two weeks; started overseas first part of May; served in the 35th Division, Company "I" 138th Infantry under Major General Joseph E. Kuhn; was engaged in Argonne battle."

"**Edward A. Ellefson** of Sargent County, born March 17th, 1896 in Sargent County; entered service March 29th, 1918; trained at Camp Dodge, Iowa for four months; started overseas the first part of August 1918; served in the 88th Division, Company "B," 350 Infantry."

"**Hilmer L. Nelson** of Rutland, born December 18th, 1894; entered service December 10th, 1917; trained at Jefferson Barracks and Kelley Field; started overseas June 30th, 1918; served in the 199th Aero Squadron, under Lieutenant Ellis; was engaged in the Meuse-Argonne battle; discharged from service June 9th, 1919."

"**Ervin V. Thornton** of Milnor, born March 1st, 1897; entered service April 21st, 1917; trained at Great Lakes two weeks and in Boston three weeks; started overseas February 1919."

"**Theodore Arvid Anderson** of Forman, born in Sargent County, June 17th, 1889; entered service July 22nd; trained at Camp Custer, Michigan, from time of entering until his death, October 14th, 1918; served in Company "E" 78th Infantry."

John Edward Davis, Edward A. Ellefson, Hilmer L. Nelson, Ervin V. Thornton, Theodore Arvid Anderson

"**Anton G. Jelinck** of Stirum, entered service September 19th, 1917; trained at Camp Dodge, Camp Pike and Camp Dix; started overseas August 26th, 1918; was on way to Verdun Front when armistice was signed; discharged March 21st, 1919."

"**Elmer Hamlet Larson** of Forman, born in Emmons, Freeborn County, Minnesota, November 28th, 1894; entered service February 5th, 1918; trained at Great Lakes, Illinois; served in Detention groups under Lieutenant John Sharpe; member Guard Company 8th Regiment until September 13th, 1918; promoted to company commander in 8th Regiment on that date; held this position while there; discharged January 27th, 1919."

"**Hjalmer W. Waldemar Nordstrom** of Milnor, born in Sargent County, October 24th, 1894; entered service June 5th, 1918; trained at Paris Island one month, San Francisco de Macoris D. R. four months." He remained in the service after the war.

"**G. Dewey Nordstrom** of Milnor, born in Sargent County, June 9th, 1898; entered service April 20th, 1917; trained at Great Lakes, Illinois; started overseas June 20th; came back and was transferred to the U.S. Navy Yard, Norfolk, Va."

"**Lyle E. Patterson** of Cogswell, born in Maxwell, Iowa, April 4th, 1900; entered service December 31st, 1917; trained at Great Lakes, Camp DeCator and Camp Logan; started overseas May 28th, 1918; serving as second class seaman."

Anton G. Jelinck, Elmer Hamlet Larson, Hjalmer W. Waldemar Nordstrom, G. Dewey Nordstrom, Lyle E. Patterson

Corporal John Louis Rehak, Leonard R. Kotchian, George Enberg, Helmer Rommundstad, Lewis Oland

"**Corporal John Louis Rehak** of Forman, born in Brainerd, Nebraska, December 15th, 1894; entered service September 5th, 1917; trained at Camp Dodge, Camp Pike and Camp Merritt; started overseas July 1st; served in the 3rd Division."

"**Leonard R. Kotchian** of Geneseo, born in Lidgerwood, North Dakota, January 1st, 1894; entered service July 22nd, 1918; trained at Camp Custer, Michigan; served in the 14th Division Company "B" 78th Infantry; discharged February 7th, 1919."

"**George Enberg** of Havana, born in Marshall County, South Dakota, May 6th, 1894; entered service August 15th, 1918; trained at Agricultural College, Fargo, North Dakota and Fort Bliss, El Paso, Texas; served in Company "B" Motor Transport Repair Unit 316, under C. L. Worth Major I. W. C. att'd to W. T. C.; discharged March 18th, 1919."

"**Helmer Romundstad** of Havana, born in Maiden, Montana, November 27th, 1890; entered service August 15th, 1918; trained at Agricultural College, Fargo, North Dakota and Fort Bliss, El Paso, Texas; served in Company "B" Motor Transport Repair Unit 316 C. L. Worth, Major I. M. C. att'd to W. T. C.; discharged March 12th, 1919."

"**Lewis Oland** of Havana, born in Marshall County, South Dakota, July 1st, 1888; entered service July 22nd, 1918; trained at Camp Dodge, Camp Johnson and Camp Upton; started overseas October 27th, 1918; served there in Field Remount Squadron 341st under Company Commander Captain George S. Taylor; discharged from service July 14th, 1919."

Sergeant Frank Bartl, William David Davis, Anton Jorgensen, Sydney I. Austin, Harry Ivan Cooper

"**Sergeant Frank Bartl** of Stirum, born in New Ulm, Minnesota, June 8th, 1897; entered service September 13th, 1916; trained at Fort Snelling, Camp Grant, Camp Cody and Camp Dix; started overseas October 20th, 1918; served in Company "C" 135th Division U. S. Infantry, under Colonel E. D. Luce."

"**William David Davis** of Cogswell, born in Cogswell, April 19th, 1892; entered service January 4th, 1918; trained at Camp Dodge three months and Camp Gordon half a month; started overseas May 1st, 1918; served in 82nd Division, Company "F" 328; was engaged in the battle of the Toul Sector, Marbosche Section, St. Mihiel, Meuse and Argonne; was discharged May 29th, 1919."

"**Anton Jorgensen** of Havana, born in Sweden, September 25th, 1889; entered service May 9th, 1918; trained at Camp Fremont, California, Camp Mills, New York and Camp Lee, Virginia; served in Company "D" 24 M. G. Bn. 8th Division under Commander Lewis R. Ryington; discharged February 13th, 1919."

"**Sydney I. Austin** of Milnor, born in 1892, in Terryville, Wisconsin; entered service April 29th, 1918; trained at Camp Dodge, Iowa, Camp Travis, Texas and Camp Mills, New York; started overseas June 1918; was engaged in the battle of St. Mihiel, Argonne, Verdun and Belleau." He stayed overseas with the Army after the war.

"**Harry Ivan Cooper** of Gwinner, born in Mankato, Minnesota, January 30th, 1892; entered service May 1st, 1917; trained at Jefferson Barracks, Mo. for four months and Benicia, California, for nineteen and one-half months; served with Engineers Infantry Ordnance and Motor Transport Corps; was discharged April 22nd, 1919."

George J. Bucher, John Wm. Barbknecht, Fred R. Ketcham, Tom Shepstad, Christian H. Fjeldsted

"**George J. Bucher** of Forman, born at Byron, Illinois, February 15th, 1891; entered service March 8th, 1918; trained at Camp Green, Charlotte, North Carolina, two months; started overseas May 10th, 1918; served in Camp De Souge, Bordeaux, France, in the 4th Division, 4th Art. Brig., 16th F. A., under Major General Hersheg; was engaged in battle of Chateau Thierry, St. Mihiel and Argonne; serving as Corporal; discharged August 5th, 1919."

"**John Wm. Barbknecht** of Havana, born in Taylor Township, Sargent County, December 1st, 1892; entered service September 5th, 1918; trained at Camp Grant, September 7th to October 26th; Base Hospital, October 26th to April 1st, when discharged."

"**Fred R. Ketcham** of Havana, born in Marshall County, South Dakota, May 14th, 1893; entered service March 29th, 1918; trained at Camp Dodge, Iowa; one month and Camp Mills, New York; started overseas May 2nd, 1918; served in the 35th Division, 138th Infantry, Company "K."

"**Tom Shepstad** of Rutland, born in Norway; entered service March 29th, 1918; trained at Camp Dodge, one month; started overseas May 2nd, 1918; served in the 35th Division, 138th Infantry, Company "M", under Captain Thompson; was engaged in battles of St. Mihiel, Meuse, Argonne, Wessling, Somedieu; discharged May 12th, 1919."

"**Christian H. Fjeldsted** of Rutland, born in Leirsund, Norway, February 21st, 1892; entered service March 29th, 1918; trained at Camp Dodge, seven weeks; Fort Leavenworth, two months and Camp Funston, three weeks; started overseas August 11th, 1918; served in Battery "C" 337th F. A. 88th Division, under General Foot; discharged January 31st, 1919."

"**Lars K. Holen** of Rutland, born in Norway, August 22nd, 1888; entered service March 29th, 1918; trained at Camp Dodge, one month; started overseas May 2nd, 1918; served in the 35th Division, 138th Infantry, Company "K", under Captain Purce; engager in battles of St. Mihiel, Meuse, Argonne, Wessling and Somedieu; discharged May 12th, 1919."

"**Christian Herman Antonsen** of Rutland, born in Norway, April 28th; entered service March 29th, 1918; trained at Camp Dodge, one month; started overseas May 2nd, 1918; served in Company "I" 138th Infantry, 35th Division, under Captain Hiccum; was engaged in battles of St. Mihiel, Meuse, Argonne, Somelieu and Westling; discharged May 12th, 1919."

"**Wayne Sides** of DeLamere, born at DeLamere, July 12th, 1899; entered service January 21st, 1918; trained at Fort Monroe and Camp Mulberry; started overseas May 28th; served in the 35th Division, 110 Trench Mortars, under Captain Manchester; engaged at Verdun and Somme; discharged May 16th, 1919."

"**Otto Emanuel Moberg** of Milnor, born in Shuman Township, Sargent County, November 1st, 1887; entered service September 19th, 1917; trained at Camp Dodge, two and one-half months, Camp Pike four months and Camp Green, one and one-half months; started overseas May 1918; serving in Division 4, Company "B" 4th Ammunition Train; was wounded sometime the first part of October and died of wounds received, October 7th, 1918."

"**Jesse B. Olson** of Lidgerwood, born in Chicago, Illinois, December 14th, 1896; entered service January 14th, 1918; trained at Fort Barrancas, Florida, six months and Camp Eustis, Va; started overseas July 17th, 1918; serving in Battery "E" 61st Artillery, C. A. C., training near Bordeaux; discharged March 6th, 1919."

Lars K. Holen, Christian Herman Antonsen, Wayne Sides, Otto Emanuel Moberg, Jessie B. Olson

"**Richard Olafson** of Havana, born at Havana, May 13th, 1890; entered service September 17th, 1917; trained at Camp Dodge, two and one-half months and Camp Pike, seven and one-half months; started overseas June 1918, serving in 2nd Division Company "C" 23rd Infantry; was engaged in battles of St. Mihiel, Blanc Mont, and Argonne; discharged August 14th, 1919."

"**William Holt** of Milnor, born in Salor, Norway, April 25th, 1894; entered service October 30th, 1918; trained at Camp Dodge, Iowa, six weeks; discharged December 12th, 1918."

"**Pvt. Towner Baird** of Cogswell, served one year with 88th Division in France."

"**J. J. O'Neil** of Forman, born at Lakefield, Minnesota, October 2nd, 1889; entered service April 11th; trained at Great Lakes; went overseas under the command of Captain W. H. Wilcox."

"**Edward J. Leach, Jr.** of Minneapolis, Minnesota, born in Havana, December 29th, 1895; entered service September 1918; trained at Fort Snelling, serving in Hospital Corp."

Richard Olafson, William Holt, Private Towner Baird, J.J. O'Neil, Edward J. Leach, Jr

Samuel J. Leach, Walter Herman Anderson, Clyde Earl Wortman, Corporal James L. Simpson, Edward Dollivar Holmes

"**Samuel J. Leach** of Havana, born November 26th, 1892, at Havana; entered service April 28th, 1917; trained at Jefferson Barracks, Fort H. G. Wright and Fort Adams; started overseas August 18th, 1917; served in Battery A. 52nd Coast Artillery Corp, under General Chamberlain; engaged in battles at Thierville, Meuse, Baleicourt, Meuse, St. Mihiel and Argonne; discharged January 25th, 1919."

"**Walter Herman Anderson** of Havana, born in Linn Grove, Iowa, July 17th, 1895; entered service January 15th, 1918; trained at Jefferson Barracks, two months; died in service, March 22nd, 1918."

"**Clyde Earl Wortman** of Havana, born in Sechlerville, Wisconsin, March 3rd, 1894; entered service June 24th, 1918; trained at Camp Dodge, five weeks and one week at Camp Mills; started overseas August 11th, 1918; served in the 88th Division, Company A 313 M. P.; contracted pneumonia and died October 11th, 1918, at Froidoo, France."

"**Corporal James L. Simpson** of Havana, born in Neuman, Illinois, May 20th, 1892; entered service April 27th, 1917; trained at Britton, South Dakota, July 15th, 1917 to September 17th, 1917 and Camp Cody until starting overseas October 1918; served in Company "D" 59th Infantry 4th Division; discharged from service August 15th, 1919."

"**Edward Dollivar Holmes** of Havana, born in Havana, February 3rd, 1896; entered service April 27th, 1917; trained at the following camps: Britton, South Dakota, July 18th, 1917 to September 17th, 1917; Camp Cody, February 4th, 1918; Del Rio, Texas, August 5th; Fort Worth, September 20th, 1918; Brownsville Dist. (Action duty) November 20th; Fort Clark from December 22nd to April 10th, 1919, when discharged as 2nd Lieutenant."

Arthur E. Berg, Harvey D. Webster, George J. Nelson, Peter Nelson, Herbert Lewis Larson

"**Arthur E. Berg** of Rutland, born in Sweden, September 7th, 1890; entered service March 29th; trained at Camp Dodge, three weeks; started overseas May 2nd; 1918; served in Company "T" 138th Infantry 35th Division, under General Wright; was engaged in the battle at the Somme Front, Vosger Milus, St. Mihiel, Meuse-Argonne; discharged May 5th, 1919."

"**Harvey D. Webster** of Cogswell, born at Livermore, Iowa, February 24th, 1896; entered service January 17th, 1918; trained at Fort Leavenworth, Kelly Field and Rockwell Field, San Diego; served in Squadron G. Air Service under command of H. Inge; discharged from service April 3rd, 1919."

"**George J. Nelson** of Angela, Montana; born in Marseilles, Illinois, December 26th, 1894; entered service May 1918; trained at Camp Lewis, Camp Kearney, California, Camp Mills; started overseas August 1918; served in Company "C" 128th Infantry; killed in action in France, October 12th, 1918."

"**Peter Nelson** of Forman, born in Allessud, Norway, August 4th, 1892; entered service March 29th, 1918; trained at Camp Dodge; started overseas April 24th, 1918; served in the 35th Division, 138th Regiment Company "L," under Captain Sodaman; discharged from service May 12th, 1919; engaged in the battles of Hilsenfirst, LeCollet, St. Mihiel, Argonne, Somme-dieux and Verdun."

"**Herbert Lewis Larson** of Havana, born in Sargent County, January 15th, 1888; entered service September 19th, 1917; trained at Camp Dodge, Iowa and Camp Pike, Arkansas; started overseas May 8th, 1918; served in the 2nd Division, 23rd Infantry Company "M"; was engaged in the battles of the Marne and Argonne; discharged from service April 12th, 1919."

"**James T. Lynch** of Havana, born in Wisconsin, December 16th, 1889; entered service February 27th, 1918; trained at Camp Dodge, Camp Upton and Camp LeSouge, France went overseas April 22nd, 1918; served in the 77th Division, Bat. A., 304th Field Artillery commanded by Captain Lyman; was engaged in the battles of Alsace-Lorraine Front, Argonne, Argonne-Meuse; discharged from service July 3rd, 1919."

"**Chas. Jackman** of Forman, born in Cayuga, October 23rd, 1895; entered service April 14th, 1917; trained at Great Lakes and Dunwoody Institute; started overseas January 20th, 1918; discharged from service March 8th, 1919."

"**Lucius R. Jackman** of Forman, born in Cayuga, September 23rd, 1893; entered service April 22nd, 1917; trained at Great Lakes, then stationed on the U.S.S. Vermont, Ohio, San Diego; discharged from service June 27th, 1919."

"**Arthur F. Person** born March 10th, 1894; entered service May 24th, 1918; trained at Camp Lewis and Camp Kearney; started overseas August 12th, 1918; was engaged in the Meuse-Argonne battle; discharged from service May 7th, 1919."

"**William E. Riley** of Geneseo, born at Havana, July 15th, 1899; entered service July 15th, 1917; started overseas December 17th, 1917; in service in France in the Toul Sector (Defensive) Cantigny Offensive, Montdidier Defensive, Soissons Offensive; was shell shocked, gassed and side sprained; discharged from service March 30th, 1919."

James T. Lynch,
Chas. Jackman,
Lucius R. Jackman,
Arthur F. Person,
William E. Riley

"**Wellington Paul Smith** of Forman, born at August 14th, 1895; entered service April 14th, 1917; trained at Great Lakes, Illinois, six days, then served on the Battleship Pennsylvania; discharged from service June 2nd, 1919."

Carl Olson (No information).

"**Fred Mercellus** of Exeter, California, born November 6th, 1896; entered service June 4th, 1918; trained at Naval Gas Engineer's School, Columbia University, New York City; served on Submarine Chaser 291, on convoy duty; discharged from service July 26th, 1919."

"**Ray F. Clapper** of Havana, born in Rockwell, Iowa, April 8th; entered service September 27th, 1918; trained at Camp Custer and Camp Dodge; served in the 14th Division Headquarters Troop; Mounted orderly under Captain James O'Connor."

"**George Hoflen** of Rutland, born in Orleans, South Dakota, December 23rd, 1893; entered service April 29th, 1918; trained at Camp Dodge and Camp Mills; started overseas August 15th, 1918; served in the 88th Division, 313th Engineer's Train under Colonel Howell; discharged from service June 15th, 1919."

Wellington Paul Smith, Carl Olson, Fred Mercellus, Ray F. Clapper, George Hoflen

"**John Joseph Waldowski** of Rutland, born in Alberta, Minnesota, April 19th, 1895; entered service July 22nd, 1918; trained at Camp Custer, Michigan; served in Company "S" 21st Engineer's; discharged December 18th, 1918."

"**Harry Pederson** of Rutland, born April 11th, 1894; entered service July 22nd, 1918; trained at Camp Custer, Michigan; died in service of pneumonia, October 16th, 1918."

"**Arthur L. Anderson** of Havana, born in Marshall County, South Dakota, May 28th, 1897; entered service May 10th, 1917; trained at Great Lakes, Illinois; started overseas February 1918; served there in the Naval Aviation and U.S.S. Leviathan."

"**John A. Stenvold** of Forman, born at Forman, May 30th, 1894; entered service August 25th, 1918; trained at Camp Lewis, Washington; served in Company "G" 75th Infantry, 13th Division; discharged from service January 25th, 1919."

"**John P. Benson** of Cogswell, born in Norway: entered service November 17th, 1917; trained at Camp Dodge, Iowa; went overseas and was engaged in the battles of the Marne, St. Mihiel, Salient-Argonne; wounded in battle of Argonne Front, September 26th, 1918, left arm, right shoulder; discharged from service April 5th, 1919."

John Joseph Waldowski, Harry Pederson, Arthur L. Anderson, John A. Stenvold, John P. Benson

Edward W. Vanderlaan, George S. Kubacki, August A. Seeman, Henry W. Seeman, George F. Vanderlaan

"**Edward W. Vanderlaan** of Cogswell; trained at Camp Dodge, Iowa; started overseas May 2nd, 1918; served in Company "M" 138th Infantry 35th Division; was engaged in the Battle of St. Mihiel, Argonne and Wesinling; discharged from service May 12th, 1919."

"**George S. Kubacki** of Geneseo, born in Great Bend, North Dakota, December 28th, 1891; entered service June 24th, 1918; trained at Camp Dodge, Iowa; served there in Company 13, 4th Bn. 163 D. B.; died at Camp Dodge, Iowa, August 30th, 1918."

"**August A. Seeman** of Cogswell, born in Jasper, Minnesota, May 20th, 1895; entered service September 12th, 1917; trained at Camp Dodge, Iowa and Camp Pike, Arkansas; started overseas June 19th, 1918; served in Company "K" 168 Infantry 42 Division; was engaged in the battle of Chateau Thierry and St. Mihiel; wounded in the battle of St. Mihiel, September 6th, 1918, on right side; discharged from service March 30th, 1919."

"**Henry W. Seeman** of Cogswell, born in Sioux City, Iowa, April 22nd, 1893; entered service August 27th, 1918; trained at Camp Lewis, Washington; served in Company "G" Regiment 75, 13th Division; discharged from service January 30th, 1919."

"**George F. Vanderlaan** of Cogswell, born November 18th, 1891; entered service September 19th, 1917; trained at Camp Dodge, Iowa and Camp Pike, Arkansas; Camp Dix, New Jersey and Camp Merritt, New Jersey; started overseas September 1st, 1918; served in Supply Company, 347 Infantry, 87th Division; discharged from service January 29th, 1919."

"**Orin Vern McNeil** born April 1st, 1895; entered service July 1917; trained at Camp Cody; started overseas June 25th, 1918; killed in action September 29th, 1918."

"**Corporal Christian D. Sundlie** of Forman, born September 29th, 1893; entered service July 22nd, 1918; trained at Camp Custer; served in the 14th Division M. G. Company 78th Infantry under Colonel McCoy; discharged from service January 7th, 1919."

"**Clarence McNeil** born April 8th, 1896; entered service September 5th, 1918; trained at Camp Grant; served in Company 36 9th Training Battalion; discharged from service January 3rd, 1919."

"**George K. Sundlie** of Forman, entered service in August; trained at Camp Lewis and Camp Prendeu; served in the Medical Corps."

"**Olaf Nundahl** of Rutland, born in Rutland, February 2nd, 1890; entered service August 26th, 1918; trained at Camp Lewis, Washington and Presidio of San Francisco, California; discharged from service July 10th, 1919."

Orin Vern McNeil, Corporal Christian D. Sundlie, Clarence McNeil, George K. Sundlie, Olaf Nundahl

"**Gust Hanson** born in Sweden, September 3rd, 1893; entered service September 19th, 1917; trained at Camp Dodge and Camp Pike; discharged from service January 29th, 1919."

"**Frank Oscar Mahrer** of Rutland, born September 19th, 1894; entered service July 22nd, 1918; trained at Camp Custer; served in the 14th Division Company "B" 78th Infantry; discharged from service February 7th, 1919."

"**George L. Randol** of Cogswell, born in Iowa, February 5th, 1899; entered service October 26th, 1917; trained at Kelly Field; started overseas January 15th, 1918; served in the 655 Aero Squadron; discharged from service May 20th, 1919."

"**Elmer Leanitie Oxley** born at Maxwell, Iowa, February 4th, 1896; entered service May 26th, 1917; trained at San Diego, California and at Norfolk, Va.; discharged August 11th, 1919."

"**Sergeant Giles Smith** born September 1st, 1898; entered service November 7th, 1917; trained at Morrison Training Camp, Morrison, Virginia; discharged from service December 24th, 1918."

Gust Hanson, Frank Oscar Mahrer, George L. Randol, Elmer Leanitie Oxley, Sergeant Giles Smith

"**Oscar C. Nubson** of Cogswell, born at Canby, Minnesota, October 20th, 1896; entered service April 17th, 1917; trained at Great Lakes; then transferred on U.S.S. Nebraska; then to U.S.S. Idaho."

"**Philip M. Englerth** of Cogswell, born in Cass County, North Dakota, May 14th; entered service June 24th, 1918; trained at Camp Dodge and Camp Mills; started overseas September 4th, 1918; served in Company I, 352nd Infantry, 88th Division; discharged June 14th, 1919."

"**Frank Z. Davenport** born at Rutland, Iowa; entered service April 13th, 1917; trained at Great Lakes, Illinois; started overseas August 8th, 1917; discharged from service August 7th, 1919."

"**Oliver A. Wells** of Forman, born in Blackhauk County, Illinois June 29th, 1893; entered service June 9th, 1918; trained at Camp Custer, Michigan; served in the 14th Ammunition Train."

"**Carl Olstad** of Rutland, born at Rutland November 29th, 1891; entered service September 5th, 1917; trained at Camp Dodge; served in Company L 352nd Infantry; discharged December 15th, 1917; on account of poor health, died from Tuberculosis July 17th, 1919."

Oscar C. Nubson,
Phillip M. Englerth,
Frank Z. Davenport,
Oliver A. Wells, Carl
Olstad

32   Susan Mary Kudelka

"**Elmer J. Nelson** born October 8th, 1895; entered service February 25th, 1918; trained at Camp Dodge, Iowa and Camp McArthur; started overseas June 30th, 1918, served in the heavy artillery; discharged from service June 16th, 1918."

"**Harold Leed DePriester** born May 5th, 1897; entered service May 1917; trained at Great Lakes, Illinois; served as 2nd class electrician C.R.O.; discharged from service August 6th, 1919."

"**Kenneth Lyman Himebaugh** of Forman, born at Forman, February 5th, 1902; entered service October 8th, 1918; trained at Paris Island, Utica, New Jersey; started overseas to St. Pedro De Mvcora, D. R., February 2nd, 1919."

"**Gustav L. Gullekson** entered service November 17th, 1917; trained at Fort Flagler; served in Bty. E. 63 C.; started overseas July 13th, 1918; discharged from service February 6th, 1919."

"**Charles Henry Cookson** of Forman, born at Rutland, November 19th, 1897; entered service December 10th, 1917; trained at Naval Training Station, San Francisco, one month; Naval Training Station, San Diego, three months; Naval Operating Base, Hampton Roads, one week; U.S.S. Alabama, nine months and Great Lakes, three weeks; discharged from service February 7th, 1919."

Elmer J. Nelson, Harold Leed DePriester, Kenneth Lyman Himebaugh, Gustav L. Gullekson, Charles Henry Cookson

History of Sargent County - Vol. 2 - 1880-1920

"**Corporal Harold O. Dyste** of Forman, born in Forman, March 11th, 1892; entered service May 29th, 1918; trained at Camp Dodge, Iowa; started overseas May 2nd, 1918; was engaged in the battle of Vosges, St. Mihiel and Argonne; discharged from service May 1st, 1919."

"**Elmer G. Enge** of Milnor, born in Shuman Township, Sargent County, May 3rd, 1894; entered service November 3rd, 1918; trained at the Agricultural College of Fargo and died there November 20th, 1918."

"**George C. Enge** of Milnor, born in Shuman Township, Sargent County, May 26th, 1892; entered service September 2nd, 1918; trained at Camp Grant, Illinois; died at Camp Grant, October 7th, 1918, of pneumonia."

"**Sergeant Viking A. Ramsing** born in Lund, Sweden; entered service September 19th, 1917; trained at Camp Dodge, Iowa; started overseas August 1st, 1918; served in Machine Gun Company 352nd Regiment, 88th Division; was engaged in the battles of Haute Alsace, Center Sector, October 12th, November 4th, 1918; discharged from service June 13th, 1919."

"**Dellie Nundahl** of Rutland, born at Perry, North Dakota, April 1st, 1893; entered service August 25th, 1918; trained at Camp Lewis and American Lake, Washington; served in the 13th Division Company "C" 213th Field Signal Battalion, under Captain De Vere Harden; discharged from service January 17th, 1919."

Corporal Harold O. Dyste, Elmer G. Enge, George C. Enge, Sergeant Viking A. Ramsing, Dellie Nundahl

Lance Emil Cooper, Oscar Benson, Jalmar Elliner Hagen, John George Lilla, Sr., Lieutenant Harry Harrison VanOrnum

"**Lance Emil Cooper** of Newark, South Dakota, born November 19th, 1895; entered service July 1918; trained at Camp Custer, Michigan; served in Headquarters Company 41st Field Artillery; discharged from service February 7th, 1919."

"**Oscar Benson** of Gwinner, born in Hensingborg, Sweden, July 18th, 1889; entered service May 24th, 1918; trained at Camp Lewis; started overseas in July; served in the Sharpshooters Company, 132nd Division; was engaged in the battle of Chateau Thierry and was gassed and wounded in hip," then sent to the Hot Springs General Hospital."

"**Jalmar Elliner Hagen** of Stirum, born at LaCrosse, Wisconsin, January 9th, 1886; entered service April 1918; trained at Camp Grant; discharged from service December 8th, 1918."

"**John George Lilla** of Stirum, born at New Ulm, Minnesota, June 7th; entered service March 29th; trained at Camp Dodge, Iowa; started overseas in April; served in the 35th Division, 128th Company; was engaged in the battles of Argonne and Mihiel; discharged from service April 1919."

"**Sr. Lieutenant Harry Harrison VanOrnum** of Minneapolis, Minnesota, born at Forman, September 28th, 1888; entered service November 1917; trained six weeks at Havall, Annapolis and three months on Battleship Nevada; discharged from service April 1919."

"**Clarence Edman Wolsted** of Cogswell, born at Harmony, Minnesota, September 4th, 1891; entered service March 29th, 1918; trained at Camp Dodge, Iowa; started overseas August 10th, 1918; served there in the 88th Division, 349th Field Hospital Company, 313 Sm. Tm., under Major Dyar; discharged from service July 30th, 1919."

"**Thomas J. Daley** of Cogswell, born at Grand Meadow, Minnesota, May 19th, 1893; entered service September 5th, 1917; trained at Camp Dodge, Iowa; started overseas August 10th, 1918; served there with the 88th Division until September 25th; transferred to Company "C" First Armp U. P., under General Bandholts; was engaged in the Meuse-Argonne battle; discharged from service July 14th, 1919."

"**Stephen Hegedus** born August 16th, 1892; entered service March 29th, 1918; trained at Camp Dodge and Fort Riley."

"**Maurice Emil Lee** of Cogswell, born at Cogswell, July 13th; entered service 1918; trained at Camp Dodge, six weeks; discharged from service in 1918."

"**Lowell M. Foster** of Milnor; entered service at Minneapolis, Minnesota; trained at Commonwealth Pier, Boston."

Clarence Edman Wolsted, Thomas J. Daley, Stephen Hegedus, Maurice Emil Lee, Lowell M. Foster

"**Corporal Percy Herbert Dyste** of Huron, South Dakota, born at Forman, July 9th, 1894; entered service March 29th, 1918; trained at Camp Dodge, three weeks; Camp Mills, Long Island, three days; started overseas May 3rd, 1918; served there in the 35th Division, Company "L" 139th Infantry, under Company Commanders Captains Haftle and Carter; was engaged in the battles of Weserling Sector, St. Mihiel, Argonne and Verdun Sector; shrapnel wound in elbow, September 28th, 1918, Meuse-Argonne Offensive; discharged May 2nd, 1919."

"**Hans N. Dyste** born June 10th, 1886; entered service September 24th, 1917; trained at Camp Dodge and Jefferson Barracks; discharged from service December 7th, 1919."

"**David Julius Rosenwater** of Milnor, born January 7th, 1882; entered service November 10th."

"**Sigurd Melvin Anderson** of Cogswell, born at Cogswell, September 20th, 1896; entered service June 23rd, 1918; trained at Hoboken, New Jersey and at Dunwoody Institute at Minneapolis."

"**Eddie McLean** of Rutland, born at Orleans, South Dakota, August 5th, 1893; entered service June 24th, 1918; trained at Camp Dodge; started overseas August 15th, 1918; served in the 88th Division Company "B" 352nd Infantry, under General Wiegel; discharged from service June 14th, 1919."

Corporal Percy Herbert Dyste, Hans N. Dyste, David Julius Rosenwater, Sigurd Melvin Anderson, Eddie McLean

Percy John Nunn, Ray Arthur Young, Rho Robinson Herring, Norris O. Anderson, Theodore Anderson

"**Percy John Nunn** of Milnor, born at Stoughton, Wisconsin, October 11th, 1897; entered service June 1st, 1918; trained at Jefferson Barracks, Mo., one month; Camp Funston, Kansas, five months; Fort Leavenworth, Kansas, three months; served in the 10th Division, 20th Regiment Company G, under General Wood; discharged from service February 11th, 1919."

"**Ray Arthur Young** of Spring Valley, Minnesota, born at Winneobogs, Minnesota, August 16th; trained at Camp Dodge, two weeks; Fort Riley, Kansas, two weeks and Fort Des Moines, seventeen months; discharged July 9th, 1919."

"**Rho Robinson Herring** born April 5th, 1896; entered service September 19th, 1917; trained at Camp Dodge, Iowa and Camp Pike, Arkansas; started overseas June 22nd, 1918; served in Company H, 23rd Infantry, Second Division; took part in the battles of St. Mihiel, Champagne and Argonne; wounded by machine gun bullet at Argonne, November 4th, 1918; discharged from service April 24th, 1919."

"**Norris O. Anderson** of Havana, born at Havana, April 3rd; entered service June 5th, 1917; trained at Philadelphia, Pennsylvania, seventeen months and Gauntanams Bay, Cuba, six months; served in Company 159, 1st Regiment."

"**Theodore Anderson** of Havana, born at Havana, June 29th; entered service August 26th, 1918; trained at St. Lewis, Washington, five months; served in the 96th Infantry, 13th Division; discharged from service January 29th, 1919."

"**Roy Chester Cooper** of Brampton, born at Brampton, May 11th, 1899; entered service June 10th, 1918; trained at Jefferson Barracks, seven days; Camp Johnson, Florida, six weeks; started overseas August 14th, 1918; served in 474th Motor Truck Company 418th Supply Train; was engaged in the battles of St. Mihiel, Argonne and Verdun; discharged from service July 15th, 1919."

"**Lyle Francis Cooper** of Brampton, born at Brampton, April 8th, 1897; entered service August 26th, 1918; trained at Camp Lewis, Washington, until discharged from service February 1st, 1919."

"**Sergeant John J. Carpenter** of Cogswell, born in South Dakota, January 21st, 1894; entered service December 13th, 1917; trained at Caruthers Field, Texas, eight months and Call Field, Texas, six months; discharged from service January 28th, 1919."

"**Martin Torgerson** born at Kerkhovan, Minnesota; trained at Fort Logan, California; served in the 23rd Machine Gun Battalion; discharged February 1st, 1919, from Camp Dodge, Iowa."

"**Sergeant Philip G. Silvernail** of Sargent County, born at Eau Claire, Wisconsin, April 13th, 1891; served in 828th Aero Squadron; started overseas August 30th, 1918."

Roy Chester Cooper, Lyle Francis Cooper, Sergeant John J. Carpenter, Martin Torgerson, Sergeant Phillip G. Silvernail

Jessie R. Silvernail, Andrew Wilhelm Stockstad, Harold Brakke, Sergeant Dwight Samuel Zimmerley, Nels Anderson

"**Jesse R. Silvernail** of Sargent County, born in Sargent County, January 21st, 1897; entered service September 13th, 1918; trained at Fort Sheridan, Illinois and Camp Grant, Illinois; discharged from service April 16th, 1919."

"**Andrew Wilhelm Stockstad** of Milnor, born in Shuman Township, Sargent County, November 3rd, 1894; entered service September 5th, 1918; trained at Camp Grant, Illinois, three weeks; Camp Hancock, Georgia, three months and Camp Dodge, Iowa, nine days; discharged from service January 9th, 1919."

"**Harold Brakke** of Sargent County, born June 18th, 1897; entered service July 9th, 1918; trained at Fort Leavenworth, Kansas; served in the U.S. Signal Corps; started overseas August 31st, 1918; was engaged in the battle of the Argonne; discharged from service June 21st, 1919."

"**Sergeant Dwight Samuel Zimmerley** of Cogswell, born at Cogswell, March 1st, 1898; entered service April 18th, 1917; trained at Kelley Field, San Antonio, Texas."

"**Nels Anderson** of Milnor, born at Milnor, June 8th, 1888; entered service September 19th, 1917; trained at Camp Dodge, Iowa, two months; Camp Pike, Arkansas, four months; Camp Mills, New York, two weeks; started overseas May 6th, 1918; served in the 4th Division Company B, 10th Machine Gun Bn., under Captain Thorpe; was engaged in the battle of the Aisne-Marne, Vesle Sector, St. Mihiel and Meuse-Argonne; discharged from service 1919."

Erick Anderson,
Charles H. Clark,
Axel B. Askerooth,
Oscar H. Johnson,
Covelia McPeak

"**Erick Anderson** of Milnor, born at Milnor, September 15th, 1895; entered service July 22nd, 1918; trained at Camp Custer, Michigan, eight months; served in the 14th Division, Supply Company, 78th Infantry, under General Hutchenson; discharged from service March 22nd, 1919."

"**Charles H. Clark** born September 6th, 1889; entered service June 30th, 1918; trained at Grand Forks, Fort Leavenworth, Kansas and Camp Dodge; served in the Signal Corps; started overseas November 5th, discharged July 5th, 1919."

"**Axel B. Askerooth** born at Cayuga; entered service March 29th, 1918; trained at Camp Dodge, Iowa; discharged May 3rd, 1919."

"**Oscar H. Johnson** born March 30th, 1892; entered service August 15th, 1918; trained at Agricultural College, Fargo, North Dakota and Fort Bliss, Texas; discharged from service March 20th, 1919."

"**Covelia McPeak** born in Virginia, October 3rd, 1896; trained at Camp Lewis, Washington; started overseas August 11th, 1918; discharged May 18th, 1919."

"**Albert C. Carlson** of Milnor, born at Berseford, South Dakota, May 10th, 1894; entered service May 24th, 1918; trained at Camp Lewis, three weeks; Camp Kearney, five weeks and Camp Mills, two weeks; started overseas August 8th, 1918; served in Company C, 128th Infantry, 32nd Division; discharged April 11th, 1919."

"**Henry George Flaseh** of Milnor, born at Sutton, Nebraska, June 9th, 1895; entered service July 22nd, 1918; trained at Camp Custer, Michigan and Camp Dodge, Iowa; discharged February 7th, 1919."

"**Corporal Frank Alphons Klinkhammer** of Cogswell, born at Ashton, Iowa, October 27th, 1891; entered service May 24th, 1918; trained at Camp Lewis, twenty days and Camp Kearney, thirty-four days; started overseas August 11th, 1918; served in the 40th Division, Company B, 158th Infantry, under General Frederic Strong; discharged from service April 29th, 1919."

"**Walter Theodore Bergquist** of Milnor, born at Duluth, Minnesota, March 8th, 1898; trained at Great Lakes from May 1917 until August 1917; Philadelphia Navy Yard for one month; then transferred to the U.S. Montana, until discharged from service May 6th, 1919."

"**Eugene C. Beron** entered service September 5th, 1918; trained at Camp Grant; discharged from service February 11th, 1919."

Albert C. Carlson, Henry George Flaseh, Corporal Frank Alphons Klinkhammer, Walter Theodore Bergquist, Eugene C. Beron

Alfred Swanson, Sergeant Richard Andrew Mahrer, Sergeant Norman Merrill Holder, Lars K. Holen, Corporal Edward Thompson

"**Alfred Swanson** born February 7th, 1891; entered service August 25th, 1918; trained at Camp Lewis, Washington, Camp Upton and Fort Benjamin; started overseas November 10th, 1918; discharged from service May 22nd, 1919."

"**Sergeant Richard Andrew Mahrer** born August 28th, 1893; entered service September 5th, 1917; trained at Camp Dodge, Iowa; started overseas August 18th, 1918; served in Artillery Battery "D" 338th, in training Camp DeSouge; Bordeaux, France; discharged from service January 17th, 1919."

"**Sergeant Norman Merrill Holder** of Forman, born at Havana, July 19th, 1895; entered service September 5th, 1917; trained at Camp Dodge, Iowa; started overseas August 16th, 1918; served in the 88th Division, 352nd Regiment Headquarters Company; discharged from service June 16th, 1919."

"**Lars K. Holen** of Rutland, born in Norway, August 22nd, 1888; entered service March 29th, 1918; trained at Camp Dodge, one month; started overseas May 2nd, 1918; served in the 35th Division, 138th Infantry, Company "K" under Captain Purce; engaged in the battles of St. Mihiel, Meuse, Argonne, Wessling, Somedieu; discharged May 12th, 1919."

"**Corporal Edward Thompson** of Rutland, born at LaCrosse, Wisconsin, March 13th, 1890; entered service June 4th, 1917; trained at Camp Cody, New Mexico and Camp Merritt, New Jersey; started overseas June 28th, 1918; served in the 90th Division, under General Allen; was engaged in the battles of St. Mihiel and Meuse-Argonne; discharged from service June 21st, 1919."

"**Albert H. Scoville** of Forman, born December 16th, 1892; entered service May 24th, 1918; trained at Camp Lewis, Washington; started overseas July 5th, 1918; served in the 91st Division M. G., Company 362nd Infantry, under Major-General Johnson; was engaged in the Argonne-Meuse battle, injured July 23rd, 1918, near Mantes, France; discharged from service May 2nd, 1919."

"**Charles Scoville** of Forman, born April 24th, 1900; entered service October 22nd, 1918; trained at the Agricultural College, Fargo, North Dakota; discharged from service December 16th, 1918."

"**Freddie J. Finn** of Cogswell, born at Alcester, South Dakota, March 23rd, 1891; entered service September 19th, 1917; trained at Camp Dodge, Camp Pike, Camp Greene and Camp Mills; started overseas May 10th, 1918; served in Company "G" 59th Infantry, 4th Division, under Captain A. D. DeBusk; was engaged in the Argonne battle, where he was killed in action August 11th, 1918."

"**Sergeant Stephen H. Yrie** of Brampton, born in Ellis, Kansas, December 25th, 1894; entered service September 19th, 1917; trained at Camp Dodge and Camp Mills; started overseas August 16th, 1918; served in Company "L" 352nd Infantry, 88th Division, under Captain Albert D. Vaughn; was engaged in Defense of Haute Marne; discharged from service June 14th, 1919."

"**2nd Lieutenant Roscoe George Montgomery** of Cogswell, born August 5th, 1891; entered service January 19th, 1918; trained at Camp Greenleaf, Georgia and at Joseph E. Johnson, Florida; served in Field Remount Squadron 367; discharged from service December 10th, 1919."

Albert H. Scoville, Charles Scoville, Freddie J. Finn, Sergeant Stephen H. Yrie, 2nd Lieutenant Roscoe George Montgomery

Bernard Nilson, Evan Nilson, Ole Hoistad, Corporal Willard H. Cook, Roland O. Sweetman

"**Bernard Nilson** of Milnor, entered service from Forman; trained at Camp Dodge; went overseas and was engaged in the Meuse-Argonne battle, where he was killed in action."

"**Evan Nilson** of Rutland, entered service and trained at Camp Dodge; went overseas and was engaged in the battles of St. Mihiel and Meuse-Argonne; discharged from service at Camp Dodge."

"**Ole Hoistad** born in Norway, December 4th, 1893; entered service August 26th, 1918; trained at Camp Lewis; served in Field Artillery; discharged from service February 5th, 1919."

"**Corporal Willard H. Cook** born August 4th, 1892; entered service June 24th, 1918; trained at Camp Dodge; started overseas August 16th, 1918; served in the 352nd Infantry, 88th Division; discharged from service June 14th, 1919."

"**Roland O. Sweetman** of Lead, South Dakota, born in Calument, Wisconsin, January 23rd, 1891; entered service May 2nd, 1918; trained at Camp Stanley, Texas, four months and Camp Travis, Texas, five months; served in the 18th (Cactus) Division, Battery "D" 54th F. A., under Captain Scott S. Hart; discharged from service February 4th, 1919."

History of Sargent County - Vol. 2 - 1880-1920   45

Hilmer L. Nelson, Sergeant Hilding Einar Safstrom, Robert W. Safstrom, Carl J. Evenson, Ole M. Evenson

"**Hilmer L. Nelson** of Rutland, born December 18th, 1894; entered service December 10th, 1917; trained at Jefferson Barracks and Kelley Field; started overseas June 30th, 1918; served in the 199th Aero Squadron, under Lieutenant Ellis; was engaged in the Meuse-Argonne battle; discharged from service June 9th, 1919."

"**Carl J. Evenson** born July 29th, 1896; entered service and trained at Camp Grant and Camp Dodge; served in Company "G" 2nd Rep. Bn.; discharged from service January 10th, 1919."

"**Ole M. Evenson** born June 14th, 1888; entered service May 2nd, 1918; trained at Fremount, California; served in Company "A" 245th M. G. Bn., 8th Division; discharged from service February 27th, 1919."

Milo Edward Nubson, Henry R. Skaarer, Walter Carl Guetschow, Bartholomew Eugene McGraw, Melvin James Carpenter

"**Milo Edward Nubson** of Cogswell, born at Canby, Minnesota, December 10th, 1892; trained at Newport, Rhode Island, nine months; Electrical School in Brooklyn, New York, three months; Gyro Compass School, Hampton Roads, Virginia; served on the U.S.S. Minnesota and on the Submarine, U.S. L1."

"**Henry R. Skaarer** born October 16th, 1895; entered service June 24th, 1918; trained at Camp Dodge and Camp Mills; started overseas August 30th, 1918; was engaged in the battle of Center Haute-Alsace; discharged from service June 13th, 1919."

"**Walter Carl Guetschow** of Milnor, born in Liberty, Wisconsin, October 29th, 1894; entered service April 29th, 1918; trained at Camp Dodge; started overseas August 1st, 1918; served in the 88th Division, 313th Engineer's Train; died in service of pneumonia October 12th, 1918."

"**Bartholomew Eugene McGraw** of Cogswell, born in Sargent County, August 22nd, 1887; entered service July 23rd, 1917; trained at Camp Greene, Camp Mills and Camp Merritt; started overseas December 15th, 1917; served in Company "M" 18th Infantry, 1st Division; was engaged in the battles of Cantigny and Soissons; wounded in left hand at Soissons; discharged from service March 4th, 1919."

"**Melvin James Carpenter** of Cogswell, born in Osborne, Iowa, December 3rd, 1889; entered service December 10th, 1917; trained at Jefferson Barracks, ten days; Fort Ogelthorp, one hundred and three days; Camp Mills, seven months; Hospital No. 1, ten days; U.S. Hospital No. 21, nine and one-half months; discharged from service September 3rd, 1919."

Arthur Percyval Olson, Corporal Raymond E. Olson, Fred Berg, Sergeant George E. Merchant, Fey Beneville Fulton

"**Arthur Percyval Olson** of Milnor, born August 7th, 1893; entered service May 26th, 1918; trained at Camp Lewis, Camp Kearney, Camp Mills and Camp Deven; started overseas August 11th, 1918; served in Company "B" of the 121st M. G. Bn., under Major Remmington; was engaged in the Meuse-Argonne battle; discharged from service May 22nd, 1919."

"**Corporal Raymond E. Olson** of Milnor, born in Sargent County; entered service April 1918; trained at Camp Dodge; started overseas August 1918; served in Company "B" 313th Engineer's 88th Division, under General Weigel; discharged from service June 1919."

"**Fred Berg** born at Mankato, Minnesota, February 15th, 1893; entered service September 5th, 1918; trained at Camp Hancock and Camp Grant; discharged from service March 24th, 1919."

"**Sergeant George E. Merchant** of Forman, born in York, North Dakota, October 17th, 1889; entered service December 2nd, 1917; trained at Kelley Field and Waco, Texas; started overseas February 26th, 1917; served in 833 Aero Repair Squadron; discharged from service December 20th, 1918."

"**Fey Beneville Fulton** of Cogswell, born in Harlem, North Dakota, September 23rd, 1895; entered service June 24th, 1918; trained at Camp Dodge, Iowa; started overseas August 15th, 1918; served in Company "K" 352nd Regiment, 88th Division, under General William Weigel; was engaged in the battle of the Alsace Front; discharged from service June 9th, 1919."

Fritz M. Seeman, Sergeant John F. Napravnik, Sergeant Elmer E. Scoville, Albert H. Reisenweber, Robert Colon Thompson

"**Fritz M. Seeman** of Cogswell, born in Jasper, Minnesota, July 25th, 1893; entered service May 24th, 1918; trained at Camp Lewis, Washington; started overseas in August 1918; served in Company "B," 128th Infantry, 32nd Division; was engaged in the Battle of the Argonne and wounded in right hand; discharged from service March 17th, 1919."

"**Sergeant John F. Napravnik** of Forman, born in Humepolid, Bohemia, December 21st, 1892; entered service August 25th, 1912; trained at Camp Lewis ten months; served in the school for bakers and cooks under command of Captain DeYoung; discharged from service June 10th, 1919."

"**Sergeant Elmer E. Scoville** of Forman, born January 1st, 1891; entered service August 9th, 1917; trained at Kelly Field, two months; San Antonio, Texas, Scott Field, Belleville, Illinois, three months; started overseas December 18th, 1917; served in the 11th Aero Service Squadron 1st Day Bombardment Group, under Colonel Bowen; was engaged in the Battle of St. Mihiel and Argonne Meuse; discharged from service May 28th, 1919."

"**Albert H. Reisenweber** of Newark, South Dakota; born December 25th, 1888; entered service June 24th, 1918; trained at Camp Dodge; started overseas August 15th, 1918; served in the 88th Division, Company "B," 352nd Infantry, under Captain Walter Shindall; discharged from service June 14th, 1919."

"**Robert Colon Thompson** of Cogswell, born at Graham, North Carolina, September 30th, 1895; entered service July 22nd, 1918; trained at Camp Custer six months; discharged from service February 7th, 1919."

"2nd **Class Seaman L. Milton Berg** of Cogswell, born in Superior, Wisconsin, December 2nd, 1898; entered service April 13th, 1917; trained at Great Lakes, Illinois; served on the U.S.S. Montana, under command of Chester Wells Captain, died there April 24th, 1918."

"**Sergeant Edwin R. Berg** of Cogswell, born at Superior, Wisconsin, November 26th, 1889; entered service July 22nd, 1918; trained at Camp Custer six months, served in the 14th Division Supply Company, 77th Infantry; discharged from service February 7th, 1919."

"**Jerry Beevar** of Grantsburg, Wisconsin, born July 30th, 1897; entered service October 22nd, 1918; trained at Camp Selby, Mississippi, four months and twenty-one days; discharged from service November 12th, 1919."

"**Ole Holt** of Milnor, born in Norway, November 2nd, 1890; entered service July 22nd, 1918; trained at Camp Custer, Michigan, served in the 14th Division, Company "A," 78th Infantry; discharged from service February 7th, 1919."

2nd Class Seaman L. Milton Berg, Sergeant Edwin R. Berg, Jerry Beevar, Ole Holt

Adolph Emil Hillestad, Captain Howard L. Saylor, M.D., Hans A. Majer, Ralph M. Winn, Hjalmar Leonard Erickson

"**Adolph Emil Hillestad** of Gwinner, born in Sargent County; entered service July 22nd, 1918; trained at Camp Custer, Michigan, thirteen months and three days; discharged from service August 26th, 1919."

"**Captain Howard L. Saylor, M.D.** born August 19th, 1873; entered service August 13th, 1917; trained at Fort Oglethorpe, Georgia; Camp McClellan and Camp Taylor; served in Medical Corps, in serum, therapy and eye, ear, nose and throat work, all at base hospitals at above camps; discharged from service May 24th, 1919."

"**Hans A. Majer** of Forman, born in Norway; entered service June 24th, 1918; trained at Camp Dodge, Iowa; started overseas August 6th, 1918; served in 352nd Infantry and was engaged in defense of Center Sector; discharged from service June 14th, 1919."

"**Ralph M. Winn** born in Jackson County, Wisconsin, August 27th, 1887; entered service March 29th, 1918; trained at Camp Dodge, Iowa; started overseas April 5th, 1918; served in Company I, 3rd Batt., 138th Regiment of Inf., 35th Division, under Major Botper; was engaged in Battle of Argonne Forest; discharged from service January 22nd, 1919."

"**Hjalmar Leonard Erickson** of Milnor, born in Milnor, March 11th, 1900; entered service October 9th, 1918; trained at Fargo College S. A. T. C.; discharged from service December 13th, 1918."

"**Martin F. Manikoski** of Geneseo, born March 25th, 1896; entered service September 19th, 1917; trained at Camp Dodge, Camp Pike, Camp Stanley and Camp Travis and Leon Springs; discharged from service May 20th, 1919."

"**Vernie Dobson** of Havana, born in Blue Earth, Minnesota, January 20th, 1895; entered service March 29th, 1918; trained at Camp Dodge, Iowa; started overseas May 2nd, 1918; served in Company K, 138th Infantry, 35th Division. Was engaged in the battles of Vosges Mts., St. Mihiel, Meuse Argonne and Somme; discharged from service May 12th, 1919."

"**Richard R. Euscher** of Stirum, born January 4th, 1893; entered service July 22nd, 1918; trained at Camp Custer, Michigan; served in Supply Company, 78th Infantry, 14th Division; discharged from service February 7th, 1919."

"**Leon Charles Glenn** of Geneseo, entered service July 1918; trained at Camp Funston, Kansas; discharged from service March 1919."

"**W. J. Sedlu** of Havana. (No other information available.)"

Martin F. Manikoski, Vernie Dobson, Richard R. Euscher, Leon Charles Glenn, W.J. Sedlu

Orin Gerald Burgeson, Paul Peter Wisnewski, Arvid Oberg, Elmer Walstead, William Bye

"**Orin Gerald Burgeson** of Milnor, born in Wisconsin, February 29th, 1892; entered service June 24th, 1918; trained at Camp Dodge, Iowa; started overseas August 17th, 1918; served in 352nd F. H. 313 Sanitary Train, 88th Division, under command of Major General William Weigel; was engaged in the battle of Haute Alsace Sector; discharged from service June 15th, 1919."

"**Paul Peter Wisnewski** of Geneseo, born at Cayuga, April 3rd, 1891; entered service February 27th, 1918; trained at Camp Dodge and at American University, Washington, D. C. Started overseas May 22nd, 1918; served in 49th 20th Infantry Forestry Regiment under Captain Thos. A. Swenney."

"**Arvid Oberg** of Gwinner, born in Halland, Sweden, September 17th, 1891; entered service September 3rd, 1918; trained at Camp Grant, Illinois; served in Company G, 5th Training Regiment; discharged from service December 9th, 1918."

"**Elmer Walstead** of Forman, born in Sargent County, July 19th, 1893; entered service September 5th, 1918; trained at Camp Grant, Camp Hancock and Camp Johnston; discharged from service March 6th, 1919."

"**William Bye** of Forman, born in St. Paul, Minnesota, September 5th, 1895; entered service June 24th, 1918; trained at Camp Dodge, Iowa; started overseas August 16th, 1918; served in the 88th Division, Company G, 302nd Infantry, under Captain Howard G. Strunk; discharged from service June 13th, 1919."

William F. Brummund, Clarence Ellsworth, Daniel Weinel, James Davis, Chas O. Weston

"**William F. Brummund** of Havana, born June 17th, 1893; entered service September 19th, 1917; trained at Camp Dodge, Camp Pike and Camp Greene; started overseas May 6th, 1918; served in the 4th Division, Company E under Major General Hershey, 58th Infantry; was engaged in the battles of Aisne Marne battle July 18th, 1918, injured in the right arm; discharged from service August 8th, 1919."

"**Clarence Ellsworth** of Havana, born August 22nd, 1890; entered service March 29th, 1918; trained at Camp Dodge, Iowa; started overseas May 2nd, 1918; served in the 138th Infantry, 85th Division; was engaged in the battles of Weserling Sector, St. Mihiel, Argonne and Verdun. Gassed in Argonne drive. Discharged from service March 30th, 1919."

"**Daniel Weinel** of Oakes, entered service May 24th, 1918; trained at Camp Lewis, Washington, three weeks and Camp Kearny, California, one month; started overseas August 14th, 1918; served in the 28th Division, 111th Infantry, Company I, under Major Hallero; was engaged in the battles of the Argonne Forest and St. Mihiel; discharged from service April 2nd, 1919."

"**James Davis** of Crete, born in Nebraska, February 15th, 1896; entered service May 24th, 1918; trained at Camp Lewis, four months; Camp Fremont, California, one month; Camp Lee, six months and Camp Dodge; served in Company D, 62nd Infantry, 8th Division, under Captain Smith; discharged from service June 19th, 1919."

"**Chas. O. Weston** of Cayuga, born in South Dakota; entered service October 20th, 1917; trained at Jefferson Barracks, Mo.; started overseas on April 8th, 1917; was engaged in the battled of Lac Noir, June 21st; St. Die, June 21st, July 1st; Frappelle Offensive, August 17th to the 21st, St. Mihiel Offensive, September 12th to the 16th; Meuse Argonne, October 11th to November 11th and with the Army of Occupation, December 1st to February 7th; discharged May 7th, 1919."

Charles F. Meyer, John Francis Dougherty, Gilmer Jorgenson, Eddie P. Larson, Sergeant Frank William Blythe

"**Charles F. Meyer** of Lidgerwood, North Dakota, born in Ida Grove, Iowa, May 22nd; entered service September 19th, 1917; trained at Camp Dodge and Camp Pike; started overseas March 6th; served in G. H. D., Company A, Headquarters Bn., under Captain Donahue; discharged from service July 12th, 1919."

"**John Francis Dougherty** of Alexandria, Minnesota, born in Green Bay, Wisconsin, July 4th, 1881; entered service March 4th, 1918; trained at Jefferson Barracks, Mo., two weeks and Fort Leavenworth, Kansas two and one-half months; started overseas June 10th, 1918; served in G. Co., Depot Signal Batt., 44th Service Co., transferred to 33rd Service Co., Signal Corps, detached to 25th Eng. on phone work, detached to A. Co., 5th Field Bn. I. C. Was engaged in the battle of Chateau Thierry with 2nd Division and gassed July 22nd, 1918, which led up to bronchitis; came home as a casual. Discharged from service March 24th, 1919."

"**Gilmer Jorgenson** of Cayuga, born in Sargent County, November 14th, 1890; entered service November 29th, 1918; trained at Camp Dodge four weeks and Long Island, New York, four weeks; started overseas May 26th, 1918; served in the 35th Division, Company G, 140th Infantry, under Captain Milligan; was engaged in the battle of the Argonne, where wounded September 30th, 1918, having left leg shot off at hip."

"**Eddie P. Larson** of Oakes, born in Madrid, Iowa, April 6th, 1896; entered service March 9th, 1918; trained at Camp Greene, North Carolina; started overseas May 7th, 1918; served in the 4th Division, Company H and later Company F; was engaged in the battles of Aisne Marne and Meaux Sector; wounded slightly in left hand at battle of Chateau Thierry, July 18th, 1918; discharged from service August 8th, 1919."

"**Sergeant Frank William Blythe** of Milnor, born October 4th, 1893; entered service July 22nd, 1918; trained at Camp Custer, Michigan; served in the 14th Division, Battery F, 40th Field Artillery, under Captain Geo. Gelispe; discharged from service February 7th, 1919."

Arthur Wesley Landreth, Allen P. Rider, Benjamin H. Henson, George C. Pieterick, Elmer William Hoppa

"**Arthur Wesley Landreth** of Cayuga, entered service March 29th, 1918; trained at Camp Dodge, Iowa; served in Company "L," 2nd Infantry, 19th Division. Discharged from service February 24th, 1919."

"**Allen P. Rider** of Cayuga, born in Emmetsburg, Md., April 22nd, 1895; entered service September 19th, 1917; trained at Camp Dodge and Camp Pike; served in the 87th Division, under General Sturgis. Discharged from service May 30th, 1919."

"**Benjamin H. Henson** of Rutland, born November 5th, 1887, in Kansas; entered service December 4th, 1917; trained at Camp Greene, North Carolina. Started overseas May 22nd, 1918; served in the 4th Division, Battery A, 13th Field Artillery under Colonel Smith; was engaged in the battles of Chateau-Thierry, St. Mihiel, and Argonne Forest. Wounded in the Argonne Forest battle, November 1st, 1918; discharged from service February 8th, 1919."

"**George C. Pieterick** of Cayuga, born in Independence, Wisconsin, November 4th, 1896; entered service May 29th, 1917; trained at Jefferson Barracks, Camp Travis, Texas and Camp Dodge, Iowa. Served in Company F, 19th Infantry, 18th Division; discharged from service February 1st, 1919."

"**Elmer William Hoppa** of Cayuga, born at Mantorville, Minnesota, June 11th, 1895; entered service July 22nd, 1918; trained at Camp Custer three months; McCook's Aviation Field three months and Camp Dodge three days; discharged from service January 25th, 1919."

Corporal Lee William Odenbritt, William Korstad, Roy Raymond Carpenter, Mehrle M. Carpenter

"**Corporal Lee William Odenbritt** of Geneseo, born June 14th, 1893; entered service January 22nd, 1918; trained at Camp Dodge, Iowa; started overseas August 14th, 1918; served in the 88th Division, Company M, 352nd Infantry and engaged in defense of Center Sector Haute. Discharged from service June 14th, 1919."

"**William Korstad** born at Henning, Minnesota; entered service May 21st, 1918; trained at Camp Lewis, Camp Grant and Camp Dodge; served in 14th Infantry Band. Discharged from service July 20th, 1919."

"**Roy Raymond Carpenter** of Cogswell, born April 12th, 1898; entered service April 13th, 1917; trained at Great Lakes, Illinois. Went overseas and served in the 4th Division, under Captain G. J. Wels, on the U.S.S. Montana. Discharged from service June 4th, 1919."

"**Mehrle M. Carpenter** of Cogswell, born in Mederville, Iowa, March 18th, 1892; entered service July 21st, 1917; trained at Camp Greene and Camp Mills. Started overseas December 14th, 1917. Served in the First Division, Company "K," 16th Infantry and Machine Gun Company, 16th Infantry and Supply Company, 16th Infantry. Was engaged in the battle of Cantigny and Meuse-Argonne. Discharged from service September 25th, 1919."

History of Sargent County - Vol. 2 - 1880-1920   57

Raymond L. Bayle, Wolf Gabriel, Oscar Stonewall Morran, Robert W. Stein, Peter Sciborski

"**Raymond L. Bayle** of McKean, Erie County, Pennsylvania, born October 19th, 1892; entered service May 31st, 1917; trained at Camp Mills one month and Camp Greene two months; Camp Merritt one week; started overseas December 15th, 1917; served in 1st Division, Company H, 26th Infantry. Was engaged in the Battle of Cantigny and wounded in left thigh by a piece of high explosive shell, June 21st, 1918. Discharged from service December 27th, 1918."

"**Wolf Gabriel** of Rutland, born in Syria, December 14th, 1894; entered service September 19th, 1917; trained at Camp Dodge, Camp Pike and Camp Merritt. Served in Company I, 348th Infantry, 87th Division. Discharged from service December 7th, 1918."

"**Oscar Stonewall Morran** of Milnor, born at Battle Lake, Minnesota, October 6th, 1891; entered service May 24th, 1918; trained at Camp Lewis, Camp Fremont and Camp Mills; served in the 8th Division, Company H, 13th U.S. Infantry, under General Helmick; discharged from service May 27th, 1919."

"**Robert W. Stein** of Cogswell, born in Richland County, North Dakota, April 13th, 1893; entered service May 20th, 1918; trained at Camp Lewis, Camp Kearney and Camp Mills. Started overseas August 12th, 1918; served in the 32nd Division, 128th Infantry, Company "B," under Lieutenant Perry. Was engaged in the Meuse-Argonne battle and slightly wounded. Discharged from service May 18th, 1919."

"**Peter Sciborski** of Geneseo, born in Poland, July 19th, 1888; entered service October 11th, 1918; trained at Vancouver Barracks; served in Spruce Division and 3rd Regiment. Discharged from service December 28th, 1918."

William F. Spaulding, Fred W. White, James T. Lynch, George Lynch, Corporal William J. Lynch

"**William F. Spaulding** born June 27th, 1892; entered service December 11th, 1917; trained at Camp Dodge, Iowa; started overseas January 17th, 1917. Was engaged in the Battle of Meuse-Argonne. Discharged from service June 29th, 1919."

"**Fred W. White** of Havana, born in Benton, Wisconsin; entered service June 5th, 1917; trained at Camp Cody, New Mexico; started overseas June 28th, 1918; served in the 33rd Division, Battery B, 123rd H. F. Company, under Captain James B. Borrit. Was engaged in the battles of St. Mihiel and Argonne. Discharged from service June 8th, 1919."

"**James T. Lynch** of Havana, born in Wisconsin, December 16th, 1889; entered service February 27th, 1918; trained at Camp Dodge, Camp Upton and Camp LeSouge, France; went overseas April 22nd, 1918; served in the 77th Division, 504th Field Artillery commanded by Captain Lyman; was engaged in the battles of Alsace-Lorraine Front, Argonne, Argonne-Meuse; discharged from service July 3rd, 1919."

"**George Lynch** of Havana, born in Kankanna, Wisconsin, February 26th, 1892; entered service August 8th, 1918; trained at Camp McArthur two weeks. Started overseas October 7th, 1918; served in Company D, 9th Infantry, Second Division. Was engaged in the Meuse-Argonne battle. Discharged from service August 14th, 1919."

"**Corporal William J. Lynch** born in Morrison, Wisconsin, May 28th, 1888; enlisted March 3rd, 1918, at New Rockford, North Dakota; trained at Fort Logan and Fort Revere; overseas July 15th, 1918; served in 71st Artillery, C. A. C. Headquarters Company."

John F. Lynch, Thomas D. Lyle, Ole J. Tisdel, Jr., Harry W. Smith, James Wesley Knapp

"**John F. Lynch** of Havana, born June 12th, 1886; entered service March 29th, 1918; trained at Camp Dodge, Camp Lewis and Camp Mills; started overseas June 28th, 1918; served in the 357th Ambulance Company, 315th Sanitary Train, 90th Division; was engaged in the St. Mihiel and Meuse-Argonne battles; discharged from service June 16th, 1919."

"**Thomas D. Lyle** of Havana, born May 24th, 1899; entered service October 2nd, 1918; trained at Grand Forks, North Dakota; served in Company "B" unit, S. A. F. C., under Captain Mark M. Dolder and Captain Wells. Discharged from service January 13th, 1919."

"**Ole J. Tisdel, Jr.** of DeLamere, entered service September 19th, 1917; trained at Camp Dodge, Camp Pike and Camp Merrit. Started overseas June 28th, 1918; served in Company "H," 23rd Infantry, 2nd Division. Was engaged in the battles of St. Mihiel, Meuse Argonne and Schampagne. Wounded in Argonne Woods October 5th and blind and deaf for two weeks. Discharged from service August 14th, 1919."

"**Harry W. Smith** of Cogswell, born in Monroe, Wisconsin, February 2nd, 1899; entered service April 14th, 1917; trained at Great Lakes, Illinois. Went overseas on the Montana, which was doing convoy duty. Discharged from service August 18th, 1919."

"**James Wesley Knapp** of Milnor, born in Egan, South Dakota, January 1st, 1890; entered service April 22nd, 1917; trained at Great Lakes, Illinois and Philadelphia. Started overseas November 15th, 1917; served in band at Greenstown, Ireland. Discharged from service March 12th, 1919."

Otto Herman Kastner, 2nd Lieutenant David Linton Vail, Axel Rudolph Gustafson, Fred H. Vanderlaan, Edward Wesley Catlett

"**Otto Herman Kastner** of Forman, born December 17th, 1898; entered service October 2nd, 1918; trained at Marine Barracks, Paris Island, S. C.; discharged from service March 5th, 1919."

"**2nd Lieutenant David Linton Vail** of Milnor, born August 14th, 1889; entered service January 6th, 1918; trained at Camp Grant, Illinois. Started overseas September 8th, 1918; served in 342nd Infantry, Company I, 86th Division, under command of General Martin. Was engaged in the Battle of Meuse. Discharged from service June 6th, 1919."

"**Axel Rudolph Gustafson** of Oakes, born in Sweden, March 23rd, 1891; entered service March 29th, 1918; trained at Camp Dodge, Iowa; started overseas May 9th, 1918; served in the 35th Division, Company "H," 138th Infantry, under Captain Pears. Was engaged in the battles of St. Mihiel, Meuse Argonne. Gassed at Wesserling Hilsenfurst. Discharged from service May 1919."

"**Fred H. Vanderlaan** of Cogswell, born in Iowa, January 9th, 1894; entered service July 22nd, 1918; trained at Camp Custer, Michigan and Camp Dodge, Iowa; served in Company "F," 78th Infantry, 14th Division, under command of P. E. Moshenrose, Captain. Discharged from service January 7th, 1919."

"**Edward Wesley Catlett** of Winnebago, Minnesota, born October 21st, 1895; entered service May 29th, 1918; trained at Camp Cody, Iowa, three weeks. Started overseas April 24th, 1918; served in 5th Army Cooks, Headquarters Troops, under Colonel Russell; was engaged in the battles of Vogs Sector and St. Mihiel Offensive. Discharged from service April 29th, 1919."

Ernest Franklin Foster, Paul Peterson, Clarence O. Williams, Corporal Selmer Fedge, Olaf Lebakken

"**Ernest Franklin Foster** of Milnor, born at Verndon Center, Minnesota, November 5th, 1895; entered service May 24th, 1918; trained at Camp Lewis three weeks and Camp Kearney five weeks; started overseas August 11th, 1918; served in the 144th M. G. B., 40th Division, 169 Company R. T. C., under command of Colonel Worth L. Section. Discharged from service October 8th, 1919."

"**Paul Peterson** of Havana, born in Britton, South Dakota; entered service September 19th, 1917; trained at Camp Dodge, Iowa and Camp Pike, Arkansas; started overseas May 6th, 1918; served in the 4th Division, 47th Infantry, Company H, under Major General Mark C. Hersey; was engaged in the battles of Aisne-Marne, St. Mihiel and Meuse-Argonne. Discharged from service September 8th, 1919."

"**Clarence O. Williams** of Milnor, entered service May 24th, 1918; trained at Camp Lewis and Vancouver Barracks. Served in the 89th Spruce Squadron. Discharged from service January 15th, 1919."

"**Corporal Selmer Fedge** of Milnor, born February 16th, 1890; entered service July 22nd, 1918; trained at Camp Custer, Michigan. Served in the 78th Infantry M. G. Company. Discharged from service February 7th, 1919."

"**Olaf Lebakken** no information available."

Sergeant Alvin E. Fedge, Carl George Ronning, Martin Gerhard Ronning, James Kellow Taylor, Eluth Johan Hanson

"**Sergeant Alvin E. Fedge** of Milnor, born October 2nd, 1894; entered service June 5th, 1917; trained at Fort Snelling, Minnesota; Camp Dodge, Iowa and Camp Cody, New Mexico. Served in the 34th Division, 68th Brigade, 135th Infantry, under command of Colonel Luce. Discharged from service February 6th, 1919."

"**Carl George Ronning** of Milnor, born September 12th, 1892; entered service May 9th, 1918; trained at Fort Logan, Camp Fremont, Camp Mills, Camp Lee and Camp Dodge. Served in the 8th Division, Company "B," 22nd Machine Gun Battalion, under Captain Albert B. Fisher. Discharged from service February 27th, 1919."

"**Martin Gerhard Ronning** of Milnor, born August 19th, 1896; trained at Camp Grant, Illinois, Camp McArthur, Texas and Camp Dodge, Iowa; served in Company G, 2nd B. N., under Captain Garret. Discharged from service December 23rd, 1918."

"**James Kellow Taylor** of Milnor, born September 12th, 1900; entered service October 9th, 1917; trained at Fargo College; served in Company A. S. A. T. C., under Ralph Mills; discharged from service December 13th, 1918."

"**Eluth Johan Hanson** of DeLamere, born February 27th, 1895; entered service September 19th, 1917; trained at Camp Dodge and Camp Pike. Discharged from service April 30th, 1919."

Henry N. Erickson, Edward E. Erickson, Sergeant Albin Gronlund, Sergeant Monroe P. Smith, Captain Henry B. Beeson, M.D.

"**Henry N. Erickson** of DeLamere, born in St. Peter, Minnesota, December 17th, 1892; entered service September 1st, 1918; trained two months in Grand Forks, North Dakota, five months in Camp Travis, Texas and three months in Charleston, South Carolina. Discharged from service June 9th, 1919."

"**Edward E. Erickson** of DeLamere, born December 12th, 1894; entered service August 25th, 1918; trained at Camp Lewis, Washington. Served in the 13th Division, 39th Field Artillery, Battery C. Discharged from service February 3rd, 1919."

"**Sergeant Albin Gronlund** of Forman, born April 4th, 1890; entered service January 10th, 1918; trained at Kelly Field, Texas; started overseas March 15th, 1918. Discharged from service April 7th, 1919."

"**Sergeant Monroe P. Smith** of Forman, born February 16th, 1898; entered service October 7th, 1917; trained at Camp Meade, Md., Barracks, Washington, D. C. and Camp Laurel, Md. Started overseas January 23rd; served in Engineer Truck Company, 23rd Engineers, under Colonel Keever. Discharged from service July 19th, 1919."

"**Captain Henry B. Beeson, M. D.** of Forman, born in Fond du Lac, Wisconsin, December 19th, 1880; entered service June 28th, 1917; trained at Fort Riley, Kansas, two months and Camp Bowie, Texas, eleven months. Started overseas in July 1918; served in the 36th Division as Division Surgeon under Colonel R. E. Ventcalf. Was engaged in Meuse Argonne Offensive, October 3rd to the 31st, 1918, suffered gas burns at Chuffle, France and in hospital as a patient for five months. Awarded Croix De Guerre with gold star and citation by General Petain. Discharged from service March 31st, 1919."

John Edstrom, William J. Hickey, Sergeant John H. Hohaus, 1st Lieutenant William Henry Payne, Charles Victor Payne

"**John Edstrom** of Milnor, born in Sweden, April 7th, 1889; entered service May 24th, 1918; trained at Camp Lewis, Washington and San Francisco, California; served in Company B, Military Police, 13th Division. Discharged from service April 7th, 1919."

"**William J. Hickey** of Havana, born in Chicago, Illinois, November 8th, 1897. Entered service May 7th, 1917; trained at Camp Cody, New Mexico. Started overseas June 20th, 1918; served in Battery E, 123rd F. A. Was engaged in the battles of St. Mihiel and Meuse-Argonne. Discharged from service June 1919."

"**Sergeant John H. Hohaus** of Forman, born in Mackesburg, Ohio, December 27th, 1881; entered service December 1st, 1917; trained at Jefferson Barracks, Kelly Field and Southern Field, Americus, Georgia. Served in 812th Aero Squadron and 237th Aero Squadron, Southern Field, under Major Walsh. Discharged from service February 4th, 1919."

"**1st Lieutenant William Henry Payne** of Milnor, born in Cherokee, Iowa, September 12th, 1888; entered service August 27th, 1917; trained at Fort Snelling, Fort Monroe and Fort Crockett. Started overseas July 14th, 1918; served in the Third Trench Mortar Battalion; was in command of Headquarters and Supply Company; served as Battalion Supply officer from time Unit was formed until demobilized. Battalion was an organization of Corps Artillery and was not assigned to any division. Discharged from service January 31st, 1919."

"**Charles Victor Payne** of Milnor, born in Cherokee, Iowa, July 22nd, 1896; entered service July 11th, 1917; trained at Camp Eaton, Sioux City, Camp Cody, New Mexico and Camp Dix, New Jersey. Started overseas September 17th, 1918; served in Medical Department, 109th Engineers, 34th Division, under command of Ben C. Everall, Major M. C. Discharged from service July 2nd, 1919."

Julius Oliver Foley, Joseph Edward Carlson, 1st Lieutenant Lewis M. Thune, Roy R. Boatman, John Agner

"**Julius Oliver Foley** of Wyndmere, North Dakota, born November 19th, 1895; entered service July 22nd, 1918; trained at Camp Custer, Michigan; served in Division Headquarters, 14th Division. Discharged from service February 11th, 1919."

"**Joseph Edward Carlson** of Forman, born June 23rd, 1894; entered service in August 1916; trained at Mare Island, California. Started overseas in February 1917;" remained in the service after the war on the U.S.S. Gregory, New York."

"**1st Lieutenant Lewis M. Thune** of DeLamere, born November 15th, 1892, in South Superior, Wisconsin. Entered service with Company B, N. D. M. G., September 7th, 1914; served at the Mexican Border from June 30th, 1916 to February 14th, 1917; arrived in France in the early part of January 1918. Assigned to Company "C," 60th Infantry, 5th Division, October 2nd, 1918 and went into action October 12th, 1918 and shot in action by a German sniper, October 14th, 1918."

"**Roy R. Boatman** of Milnor, born in Oakland, Iowa, August 1st, 1887; entered service April 29th, 1918; trained at Camp Dodge, Iowa and Camp Travis. Started overseas June 20th, 1918; served in Company F, 358th Infantry, 90th Division. Was engaged in the battle of St. Mihiel, where wounded by a machine gun bullet through the left arm, September 15th, 1918. Discharged from service August 5th, 1919."

"**John Agner** of Gwinner, born December 20th, 1890; entered service August 8th, 1918; trained at Jefferson Barracks, Waco, Texas and Camp Merrit, New Jersey. Started overseas August 20th, 1918; served in 2nd Division, Company "K." Was engaged in Meuse-Argonne Drive, November 4th, 1918, where wounded in the right shoulder; discharged from service April 2nd, 1919."

"**Boyd Stewart Phelps** of Milnor, born November 16th, 1892; entered service March 2nd, 1918; trained at Camp Dodge and Camp Logan. Started overseas May 10th, 1918; served in the 33rd Division, under Major General George Belhr, was engaged in the battles of Meuse-Argonne, Verdun. Discharged from service June 2nd, 1919."

"**Carl Nelson** of Milnor, born January 22nd, 1896; entered service March 8th, 1918; trained at Camp Greene, North Carolina. Started overseas May 10th, 1918; served in Battery A, 16th Field Artillery, 4th Division; was engaged in the Vesle Offensive, St. Mihiel, Argonne and Toul Sector. Discharged from service August 5th, 1919."

"**Corporal Lloyd Bell** of Forman, born August 21st, 1892; entered service December 1917; trained at Jefferson Barracks, Kelly Field, Texas, Camp Hancock and Camp Merrit. Started overseas March 4th, 1918; served in 15th Company, 2nd Division under Harry Payne; discharged from service June 15th, 1919."

"**Sigfrid Benson** of Cogswell, born in Sweden; entered service June 24th, 1918; trained at Camp Dodge, Iowa; started overseas August 10th, 1918; served in the 88th Division, 352nd Infantry, Company "B" under Major General W. Wiegell; was engaged in the Battle of Haute Alsace; discharged from service June 14th, 1919."

"**Harold Randol** no information available."

Boyd Stewart Phelps, Carl Nelson, Corporal Lloyd Bell, Sigfrid Benson, Harold Randol

"**Iver Gronlund** of Forman, born June 27th, 1894; entered service June 15th, 1918; trained at Fort Benjamin and Camp Shelby. Started overseas October 6th, 1918. Discharged from service January 22nd, 1919."

"**Oscar Wahlund** of Forman, born November 7th, 1896; entered service March 23rd, 1918; trained at Fort Leavenworth, Camp Merrit and Camp Dodge; started overseas June 10th, 1918; was engaged in the Meuse-Argonne offensive and Somme offensive; discharged from service June 2nd, 1919."

"**Lewis B. Johnson** of Havana, born November 25th, 1892; entered service July 22nd, 1918; trained at Camp Dodge, Iowa. Discharged from service December 19th, 1918."

"**John H. Brummond** of Havana, entered service August 25th, 1919; trained at Camp Lewis; served in the school for bakers and cooks, under Captain D. Young. Discharged from service December 31st, 1918."

"**Sergeant Melfin O. Glorvick** of Forman, born November 21st, 1893; entered service August 8th, 1918; trained at Jefferson Barracks, Mo., Camp Hancock, Georgia and G. H. No. 19, Otein, North Carolina, eight months in reconstruction service. Discharged from service July 18th, 1919."

Iver Gronlund, Oscar Wahlund, Lewis B. Johnson, John H. Brummond, Sergeant Melfin O. Glorvick

Corporal Henry L. Mahrer, Sergeant Clinton DeWitt Baker, Ransom A. Barnes, Corporal Carl Victor Eklund, Sergeant Emmett Francis McGraw

"**Corporal Henry L. Mahrer** of Rutland, born February 12th, 1893; entered service March 29th, 1918; served with Company "H," 2nd Infantry; discharged from service June 5th, 1919."

"**Sergeant Clinton DeWitt Baker** of Forman, born July 2nd, 1892; entered service April 26th, 1917; trained at Camp Cody, New Mexico, Del Rio, Texas, Camp Bowie, Fort Worth, Texas and Fort Sill, Oklahoma; served in the 51st F. A. Band, Fort Sill, Oklahoma, under Colonel Phillips. Discharged from service February 4th, 1919."

"**Ransom A. Barnes** of Milnor, born May 9th, 1894; entered service September 9th, 1917; trained at Camp Pike, Camp Dodge and Camp Merrit. Started overseas June 22nd, 1918; served in 2nd Company, 23rd Infantry, under Major General June. Was engaged in the battles of St. Mihiel and Meuse-Argonne. Discharged from service August 14th, 1919."

"**Corporal Carl Victor Eklund** of Forman, born in Borgviks Bruk, Sweden, July 18th, 1890; entered service July 22nd, 1918; trained at Camp Custer, Michigan. Served in the 14th Division Machine Gun Company, 78th Infantry under E. E. Major, Captain. Discharged from service February 7th, 1919."

"**Sergeant Emmett Francis McGraw** of Forman, born in Cogswell, December 28th, 1893; entered service September 4th, 1917; trained at Camp Lewis, Washington; served in 91st Division, Company D, 361st Infantry. Transferred to Company F, 316th Engineers, later to Company 28, 166th Dep. Brig. Discharged from service January 23rd, 1919."

History of Sargent County - Vol. 2 - 1880-1920

Matt Gardner, John F. Lynch, John Kuczyncki, Eddie Johnson, Captain Charles Ernest Howard, M.D.

"**Matt Gardner** of Forman, born in Norway, December 9th, 1893; entered service April 29th, 1918; trained at Camp Dodge, Camp Travis and Camp Mills; started overseas June 29th, 1918; served in the 90th Division, under Battery Commander Captain Connor. Discharged from service June 6th, 1919."

"**John F. Lynch** of Havana, born June 12th, 1886; entered service March 29th, 1918; trained at Camp Dodge, Camp Lewis and Camp Mills. Started overseas June 28th, 1918 served in the 357th Ambulance Company, 315th Sanitary Train, 90th Division. Was engaged in the St. Mihiel and Meuse-Argonne battles. Discharged from service June 16th, 1919."

"**John Kuczyneki** of Geneseo, entered service March 29th, 1918; served in 43rd Division, Company C, Transportation Corps. Started overseas July 14th, 1918. Discharged June 15th, 1919."

"**Eddie Johnson** of Rutland, born September 18th, 1895; entered service April 5th, 1918; trained at Great Lakes, Illinois, four weeks. Served on Battle Ship Georgia. Discharged from service September 15th, 1919."

"**Captain Charles Ernest Howard, M. D.** of Cogswell, born at Bloomington, Wisconsin; enlisted June 25th, 1917; trained at Camp Cody, Deming, New Mexico and Camp Dix. Started overseas September 12th, 1918. Was engaged in battle of Meuse-Argonne; was with Army of Occupation in Berncastel, Germany. Served in 34th Division, 109th Sanitary Train. Commanded 135th Ambulance Company. Later transferred to 90th Division. Ambulance Company 358. Discharged from Camp Dodge, June 17th, 1919."

"**Emil N. Newman** enlisted at Milnor, June 6th, 1918. Served in Company G, 20th Infantry, 10th Division. Died in service. (No more could be learned of his activities.)"

70 *Susan Mary Kudelka*

The following is a list of men from Sargent County, who were in the service during World War I. No pictures or other information could be obtained on these men.

Ahls, Henry	Hansen, Louis	Opsahl, Melvin H.
Alfson, Leon	Helmers, J. J.	O'Conner, Henry
Anderson, Carl E.	Hemmington, Robert B.	Okeson, Ernest A.
Anderson, Gabriel	Herman, Eddie	Omalley, Edward P.
Anderson, Gustav A.	Hersgard, Alvin M.	Orn, Chas.
Anderson, Isaac	Hersgard, Ludvick C.	Parker, Lawrence
Anderson, Melvin H.	Hickey, Edward J.	Paulson, Carl
Anderson, Nils	Holmes, Morris P.	Pease, Leroy
Armstead, John	Holmstrom, Arthur	Pederson, Martin
Ash, John H.	Horstad, Edwin	Pearson, Willie
Ashley, J. H.	Hanson, Louis	Perrow, Joe
Askildson, Jacob	Hubert, Albert L.	Peterson, Carl E.
Barta, Otto C.	Hunt, Fred G.	Peterson, Emil
Bandelow, Ernest	Iverson, Roy J.	Peterson, Geo. E.
Beiersdorf, Otto W.	Jackson, Joseph	Peterson, Palmer
Berger, Louis O.	Jahnke, Hergert C.	Peterson, Theo.
Bervin, Nels W.	Janson, Severt	Peterson, Victor E.
Borchardt, L.	Jensen, Andrew C.	Prindell, William C.
Borg, Chas. H.	Jensen, Jacob	Quint, Carrol
Blash, Joseph E.	Johnson, Axel E.	Rayburn, Chas. H.
Brabec, Frank J.	Johnson, Calvin J.	Rodlund, Oscar T.
Brown, John	Johnson, Eddie	Rozell, Michial
Buen, Willie	Johnson, Oscar	Seeman, Ernest W.
Byers, William M.	Johnson, Riner	Severinson, H. T.
Cusick, Leo	Johnson, Willie C.	Sedler, Walter
Cameron, Mitchell C.	Johnson, Earl Von	Scharff, Willie
Connell, Elmer W.	Johnson, Albert J.	Sherigan, Harry
Cole, Louis R.	Karas, Edward	Shirley, Jasper
Carlson, Fritz B.	Karls, George	Sinclair, John P.
Casey, Guy W.	Kelly, Gregory	Smith, Arthur
Christianson, Harry	Kranda, John J.	Smith, Henry
Carlsen, Garfield L.	Kranlund, Karl H.	Smith, John
Carlson, Albin G.	Kramer, Henry J.	Stein, Louis John

Cole, Arthur E.
Coleman, Lysle
Crawford, Lewis C.
Crayne, Jasper Newell
Danielson, M.
Davis, Guy W.
DeWeirt, Dick
Dittle, Ray
Dockstatter, R.
Dunning, Walter M.
Dversdahl, Ole
Edblom, Harry C.
Egramyer, Geo. W.
Eidall, Geo. A.
Ekman, Ole
Ellsworth, Forrest G.
Erb, Charles
Erb, Leonard
Eving, Mitchell
Farran, Lester W.
Finch, George R.
Flick, Martin E.
Forsberg, Olaf
Foster, Edgar E.
Freeman, Frank H.
Gardner, Math
George, Robert A.
Gilbertson, Bennie
Granlund, Oscar
Grover, Hayden L.
Hamel, Warren O.

Kroken, Ole
Kriesel, Edward W.
Lagred, Edward T.
Lanning, Leory
Larson, Ole
Lavik, Rudolf
Lavik, Ingvald
Lee, Thomas A.
Lehman, Chas.
Loutzenhiser, Chas
Lucy, Daniel
Lukas, Walter
Mardyk, Frank
McPhail, Clarence
Mielke, Julius
Miller, Leroy
Morgan, Robert
Melewicz, Stanley
Miller, Fred F.
Neilson, George A.
Nelson, Albert J.
Nelson, Oscar
Niedermialk, Mike
Novotny, Alias
Noyes, Jesse R.
Nubson, Nels
Oland, Knute
Olson, Andrew
Olson, Carl J.
Olson, Edwin T.
Olson, Ingvald[2]

Stein, Emil A.
Stuart, Louis
Spanton, Arthur
Sullivan, Lewis T.
Sullivan, William
Sund, Olof
Summerfield, Louis
Tvedt, Johanes O.
Tuscow, C. A.
Vortair, Sam
Vculek, Lee
VanVlett, Robert

---

[1] D. Clayton James and Anne Sharp Wells, *America and the Great War 1914-1920* (Wheeling, Illinois: Harlan Davidson, Inc., 1998), 27-33.

[2] All information on men in Sargent County that participated in World War I from: Miles E. Reinhart, assisted by Albert Scovile, *Sargent County In The World War* (Forman, 1919)

CHAPTER 3

Civil War Veterans

The following is a list of Civil War and Spanish War Veterans in Sargent County. The list was compiled at the end of World War I.

"**Private William H. Bowser** born in Ligonier, West Morland County, Pennsylvania; enlisted May the first, 1861, for three month service; re-enlisted August the second, 1861, for three years; re-enlisted again, the 14th of August, 1861, for the duration of the war; discharged the fourteenth day of August, 1865; was engaged in the first battle of Bull Run, engaged in several and numerous skirmishes; was in battle of Gettysburg, while again, engaged in several notable battles in Pennsylvania and Virginia; nine months in the famous Libby Prison."

"**Job D. Lewis** a private of Captain John H. Folks, Company F, 26th Regiment of Illinois; infantry volunteers who were enrolled on the 6th day of August, one thousand eight hundred and sixty one to serve three years during the war. Discharged from the service of the United States, the thirty-first day of December, 1863, at Scotts Boro, Alabama, by reason of re-enlistment in Veteran Volunteers Service. Given at Scotts Boro, Alabama, the thirty first day of December 1863."

"**Jeremiah Preble** of Rutland, born in Maine, May 27th, 1848; trained at Madison, Wisconsin, one week; served in Company A, 12th Wisconsin Infantry, 3rd Division, 17th Army Corps, under Captain Reynolds; discharged from service July 16th, 1865."

"**John Hermonson** of Lidgerwood, born in Norway, January 29th, 1846; entered service May 17th, 1864; trained Davenport, Iowa; served in Company F, 46th Regiment of Iowa Volunteers; discharged from service September 23rd, 1864."

"**Wilford Herrick** born in Allen County, Indiana, January 1st, 1846; entered service January 18th, 1864; served in 3rd Regiment Wisconsin Cavalry; discharged from service July 21st, 1864."

History of Sargent County - Vol. 2 - 1880-1920

Civil War Veterans - Private William H. Bowser, Job D. Lewis, Jeremiah Preble, John Hermonson, Wilford Herrick, Jay Saunders, Sergeant John J. Wisnewski and Burton L. Bierce.

"**Jay Saunders** of Rutland, born May 20th, 1837; entered service August 7th, 1862; trained at Dockets Harbor, New York; served in the 5th Regiment New York Heavy Artillery, under Captain Clark; discharged from service July 1865."

Spanish War Veterans

"**Sergeant John J. Wisnewski** of Geneseo, born June 2nd, 1873 in Pittsburgh, Pennsylvania; entered service May 6th, 1898; trained at Camp Lytle; served in the 3rd U.S. Troop H, 2nd Division; discharged from service September 22nd, 1898."

"**Burton L. Bierce** born at Iola, Wisconsin on May 30th, 1868; entered service April 26th, two days after the celebration and was in camp at Chattanooga and Nashville, Tennessee; Chicamauga Park, Alabama and Anniston, Alabama, being in the service nearly a year in the 3rd Tennessee Volunteer Infantry; part of the time being corporal; worked as printer in Wisconsin, Michigan and served as editor on papers in Wisconsin, Tennessee and Arkansas." Was later editor of *The Union* at Havana.[1]

---

[1] All information on Civil War and Spanish War Veterans from: Miles E. Reinhart, assisted by Albert Scovile, *Sargent County In The World War* (Forman, 1919), 45.

CHAPTER 4

Sargent County Fair

Most everyone from Sargent County has memories of going to the annual Sargent County Fair in Forman. The first annual Sargent County Fair was held on October 9th to the 11th, 1918. The fair was advertised as "Over the Top at the Sargent County Fair at Forman." The stated location of the fair was to be south of the Soo Depot or in the same area that the fair is held today. The first Soo Depot was on the east side of Forman near present day Linda Reisenweber's house. The fair was held in three large tents. The first year, a significant amount of attention was given to the Women's department. Numerous organizations, with special attention given to the Red Cross had competitive exhibits at the fair. Special interest was given to canned food exhibits. At that time, Sargent County was second in the state in canning demonstrations. The County also had first and second prizewinners in the state corn contest for the Boys and Girls clubs. County Agent Greenwood was in charge of the agricultural exhibits at the fair and Livy Johnson, president of the Sargent County Livestock Breeders' association and well-known breeder of Aberdeen-Angus cattle, was in charge of the livestock department.[1]

The following is a list of committees at the first Sargent County Fair. The township chairmen were: "Louis Besuchit, Southwest; J. D. Ames and O. W. Foust, Jackson; P. E. Pederson and Henry Kraft, Verner; A. G. Kennedy, Denver; John Hove and John Stout, Brampton; J. D. Randell and Julis Wolstad, Sargent; Livy Johnson and A.W. Larse, Harlem; John McDermert and A. J. Robinson, Vivian; J. P. Williamson and E. E. Walker, Taylor; Chas. Hewitt and Chas. Rehak, Forman; A. E. Stevens, White Stone Hill; Tyler O'Neil, Bowen; Charley Christenson and Chas. Goltz, Weber; Carl Lilja and Hans Dyste, Rutland; James Lanxon and B. E. Johnson, Dunbar; M. O. Matson and J. E. Miller, Willey; Dave Nickeson, Tewaukon; Andrew

Hoflen, Ransom; J. O. Nordstrom and Henning Swanson, Shuman; Logan Stanley and Peter Christenson, Milnor; Peter Knudson, Marboe; Frank Riba and Peter Weber, Kingston; B. D. Williams, Herman; Dave Marquette and Henry Foley, Hall."

The following were named as "assistant superintendents of the women's work at the fair. Mrs. R. L. Himebaugh has charge of this department: Mrs. Livy Johnson, Cogswell; Mrs. Geo. Flemer, Milnor; Mrs. John Bussey, Havana; Mrs. E. F. Ross, Cayuga; Mrs. C. H. Nygaard, DeLamere; Mrs. M. S. Anderson, Stirum."

At the first fair, the three highest winners in the Boys and Girls Club work, from the following projects, corn, potatoes, garden canning, poultry, pigs, baking and sewing received a free trip to Fargo to attend Boys and Girls institute. On account of the war, fancy work exhibits were dispensed with.[2]

The first fair was advertised as Three Continuous Days of Joy at the Sargent County Fair. The fair included races, baseball, bands, open-air vaudeville exhibits and a bowery dance and many other activities. They also advertised agricultural and livestock exhibits.[3] Several leading educators of the state also gave lectures and demonstrations at the fair. The presentations were advertised as a worthy feature every progressive farmer in the county would want to attend. Those that gave lectures were:

Professor H. L. Bolley of the Agricultural College. He was at the fair on October 10th and took samples from all seeds shown at the fair and had the seeds tested at the Pure Seed Laboratory. Mr. Bolley later furnished a report to those that attended his lectures.

Dr. Don McMahon, State Veterinarian Specialist of the Extension Department was at the fair on October 10th and 11th to answer questions regarding livestock, including demonstrations relating to blackleg; restraint of farm animals; minor operations of interest to Livestock men; unsoundness of horses; docking lambs; dehorning and castrating pigs, lambs and calves.

Mrs. O.A. Barton, Assistant State Club Leader of the Extension Department was at the fair all three days and was in charge of judging poultry. She also gave advice about the raising of poultry for pleasure or profit. Mrs. Barton was one of the best poultry experts in the

76 *Susan Mary Kudelka*

northwest.

Miss Inez Hobart, Assistant Home Demonstration Agent for North Dakota was also in attendance all three days with an exhibit and a demonstration in Home Economics. This was advertised as an interest to all women who appreciated the importance of the home.

The Boys and Girls Club Work Exhibit was promoted as a source of interest to the coming generation who are helping to Win the War, under the banner of more and better pigs, canning, corn, poultry, gardening, bread, baking and similar subjects.

The Little Giant Amusement company, which was one of the big attractions at the Richland County Fair at Wahpeton the week before the Sargent County Fair was also advertised as a big attraction at the first fair. The company carried a $10,000 merry-go-'round, a Ferris wheel and four tent shows. In addition, the combination of Burtinos and Shattucks, a well-know vaudeville act was also at the fair. [4]

The Second Annual Sargent County Fair

By September of 1919, the fair grounds were undergoing improvements for the upcoming fair in October of that year. They erected a number of buildings, had an artesian well dug, trimmed up the grounds and built fences.

The fair board again had the Little Giant Amusement Company and in addition there was an acrobatic and trapeze act. There were of course, the usual agricultural and livestock exhibits. A band from Wahpeton also furnished music for a dance held on the first night of the fair.

The Third Annual Sargent County Fair

Among the attractions was the noted Indian Chief Bow Arrow, who performed a high wire, Barney Zimmerly one of the best aviators in the county gave nerve thrilling airplane exhibits and Field's Greater Shows furnished entertainment for the whole family. A new women's building and a poultry building were also constructed for the fair.[5] Due to inclement weather, during the first two days of the fair, it was extended three more days.[6]

The Sargent County Fairgrounds in the 1920s.

A painting of an early Sargent County Fair.

---

[1] *Sargent County News*, 16 August 1918.
[2] Committees Named for County Fair, *Sargent County News*, 30 August 1918.
[3] *Sargent County News*, 20 September 1918.
[4] *Sargent County News*, 27 September 1918.
[5] *Sargent County News*, 17 September 1920.
[6] *Sargent County News*, 1 October 1920.

CHAPTER 5

Forman

The original town site of Forman, the northeast quarter of Section 1, Township 130, Range 56, was "filed on by Beil Truesdell, a soldier in the War of the Rebellion, under the Soldier Additional Homestead Right. Shortly afterward, he died, the rights going to George H. Truesdell, minor orphan son. The Receivers Receipt was granted July 20th, 1883 and on the same day, a warranty deed was granted to Colonel C.H. Forman."

"On July 26th, 1883, Mr. Forman had a survey began, platting the original town site of Forman on this forty acre tract. The remaining

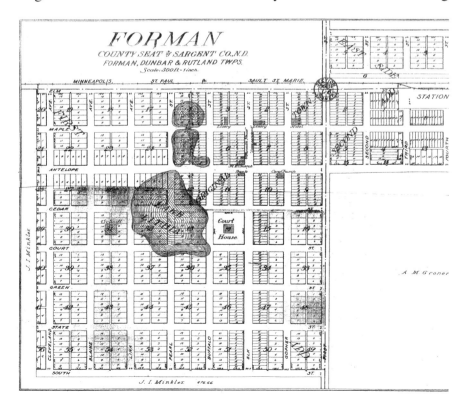

History of Sargent County - Vol. 2 - 1880-1920

one hundred and twenty acres of the northeast ° of Section 1 was filed on by William H. Groff, a son in law of Colonel Forman, and the following year, June 26th, 1884, Mr. Groff deeded this land to Mr. Forman and this, the First Addition to the Town of Forman, was platted in August, 1884."

"In 1884 Randolph Holding bought ten acres in the northeast corner of the northwest quarter of Section 6, Township 130, Range 55, from Jim Pericle, who had homesteaded it. In October, 1884, Mr. Holding had this ten acre tract platted and it became the Second Addition to the Town of Forman."

"On May 20th, 1889, the County Commissioners passed a resolution, declaring the Town of Forman duly incorporated. The territory included in this incorporation was then all of the northeast quarter of Section 1, Township 130, Range 56 and all of the northwest quarter of Section 6, Township 130, Range 55."

"On April 12th, 1889, the East Side Addition of the Town of Forman was platted. This land at that time was owned by the Pacific Land Company."

"The Gardners Addition was platted by H.O. Gardner in 1928, and is located in the southeast quarter of Section 36, Township 131, Range 56."[1]

Colonel Cornelius Hagerman Forman

Colonel C. H. Forman was born in St. Johns, New Brunswick, July 15th, 1828. After completing school he engaged in business in Hamilton, Ontario, until 1856. He then "moved to Brantford, Ontario, where he was also engaged in business and farming until 1872, at which time he went to Michigan, where, together with his brother, he founded the town of Forman, Michigan. Here he was engaged in the manufacture of lumber until 1882."[2] In his earliest years, Colonel Forman "served in a military regiment at Brampton, Ontario." "He always walked with the military bearing he had acquired in his youth in spite of the fact that he lost a leg in a train accident while he still lived in Canada and he required an artificial leg."[3]

Colonel Forman married Adeline Kelly of Kelvin, Ontario in 1851. They had seven children, "Elizabeth (Groff), Harry W. Forman, Mary

(Purdy), Lida (Gilborne), Clifton and Clyde. One son, Jesse, died in Michigan at the age of twenty-six. All of his children were born elsewhere, but lived in Forman at least for a time." Harry and his wife, Minnie, raised a family in Forman and lived there all their lives.[4] "In April, 1882, Mr. Forman, at the age of fifty-five, with his two sons, Clifton and Harry; daughters, Mrs. Elizabeth Groff, Mary Ann McDermand and Linda; sons in law, William H. Groff and Geo. McDermand and a hired man arrived in Fargo, Dakota Territory. Claude Groff, then a boy of five, states as follows: "My Recollection of the trip in covered wagons from Fargo to Sargent County is very vivid. The wild game was incredibly plentiful, there were no game laws and the men of our party shot all we could eat, some were near what is now the town of Gwinner; they also shot two antelope."[5]

"When Colonel Forman decided to build a town, he realized he would need some help. He went back to Michigan to a town that bore his name and talked several friends and relatives into coming back with him. He returned with several wealthy men. The group included, William Forman, his son, Harry Forman, A Wells, William Hudson, William Silverthorne, E. W. Bowen, G. C. Lilly, C. W. Sprague, W. T. Mullen and H. L. VanOrnum. These were the first active settlers of the town."

In 1883, lots in town sold for fifty to one hundred dollars depending on the location. Colonel Forman returned to Michigan in 1883 and brought three thousand feet of pine lumber back to Forman with him. He built a large home for himself at the corner of Maple and 2nd Street.[6]

"Once Mr. Forman secured and platted the town site of Forman, in July 1883, he built a house for himself in Lot 1, Block 7, which was the first building in the town of Forman. The same year he built a hotel on Lot 1, Block 6, which he called the Midland House; a store building on Lot 12, Block 13, known as Forman & Groff, and managed by W. H. Groff, and two other store buildings, on Lot 9, Block 6, and one on Lot 16, Block 7. A blacksmith shop was opened by Charles Moore on Lot 13, Block 8, and a saloon, known as The Frolic was opened by Frank Maxson in one room of the Midland House."[7]

Colonel Forman "served twenty-six years as town clerk, twenty years as justice of the peace, twelve years as township supervisor. In politics he was a Republican. He was a staunch member of the Congregational Church. He had given the land on which the church was built and a generous amount of money to help with the building."

"Mrs. C.H. Forman died at the age of sixty-six in February 1895. She had a severe stroke. After the death of his wife, the Colonel spent most of his years in the home of his son, Harry, both at their farm home and later in Forman. Colonel Forman lived to be very old. He was poor in his final years, he had spent all of this money. He had come from Michigan a very wealthy man for that time, some reports put it at from $50,000 to $100,000." "About two years before his death, he suffered a stroke from which he was paralyzed until his death. He died March 12th, 1924. His funeral services were held in the Congregational church. The officiating minister was Reverend A.O. Prior. He spoke from Job 6:26. At the funeral, the school children honored him by marching from the schoolhouse to the church and standing outside at attention on a cold blustery day while the church bell sadly tolled ninety-six times. Many of the young children

Colonel C.H. Forman is pictured with his family; from left: Harry, Lizzie, Colonel Forman, Lida and Mary Ann.

called him "Goppy" Forman. His nickname came from his grandchildren and no doubt a youngster's effort to say grandpa. His grandchildren who lived in Forman were: Clyde, Seth, Cornelius (Neil), Una, Naomi (Oma) and Ray."[8]

Colonel Forman is pictured with three generations. Colonel Forman in the center, is flanked on the right by his son, Harry and on the left by Harry's son, Ray.

Colonel Forman's grandsons, from left: Neil, Clyde, Seth and Ray. All are sons of Harry Forman.

Colonel Forman's home, later sold to the Mullins Family, it is now torn down. It was located to the south of Seavert's Auto Service.

Early Businesses in Forman

"By 1889, the following businesses were flourishing in Forman. One bank, one railroad, three hotels, a S.V. Camp, one paint shop, five law offices, one drug store, the county seat, a G.A.R. Post, one barber shop, two newspapers, two general stores, two livery barns, a population of three hundred, one hardware store, two butcher shops, one furniture store, a IOGT Lodge, a two thousand five hundred dollar school, two blacksmith shops, three machine depots, one confectionary store, one dentist office, an AF and AM Lodge, one jewelry store, money order post office, a fine courthouse, one physician and surgeon, one clothing store, one elevator, one millinery and dressmaking store, one flat house (grain storage), three justices of the peace, one lumber, coal and brick yard, one feed store and one mill."

In the first year or so, several hotels were built, because of the new settlers arriving. In addition law offices and real estate offices were built, because so many homesteads were being proved up. Many businesses were also moved into town. Dyste's moved from Rutland, as did Steimke and Claus Evenson. Hurly's Store came from Dunbar,

84   *Susan Mary Kudelka*

as did several other buildings and at least two buildings came from Harlem.[9]

Many new settlers and businessmen came to Forman in the early years of its history. Here is a list of some of them: "The following is a list of the early pioneers with the date of arrival, if it is known and their occupation: Mr. Fish, farmer; Col. C. H. Forman, 1882, Merchant and Land Owner: Harry Forman, 1882, farmer; W. C. Forman, 1882, Farmer and Postmaster: William Lillywhite, farmer; William Baird, farmer; L. A. Page, farmer; F. A. Purdy, farmer; Billy Ballard, Negro from the South, Farmer; Frank Zimmerly, farmer, L. A. Hohaus, 1885, farmer, George Hohaus, 1885, farmer, John Calvert, farmer; John Davis, farmer; Carl Crandall, farmer; William Groff, merchant; George McDermott, merchant and hotel manager; James Thompson, farmer; Mr. McGregor, farmer; Frank Argersinger, Livery Stable; James C. Brandt, farm machinery and farmer; A. C. Brooks, 1885, farmer; Daniel Covey, 1885, farmer and carpenter; N. H. Dyste, 1885, merchant; J. H. Dyste, 1885, merchant; E. M. Fjelstad, 1884, farmer; A. E. Land, 1883, farmer; Charles M. Scoville, 1885, Land and Loans; Edward Anderson, 1885, farmer; Dr. Holloran, 1888, physician; J. D. Vail, 1888, bank cashier; L. V. Babcock, 1888, bank cashier; W. S. Baker, 1888, merchant; Alf Ellsworth, 1885, newspaper; J. E. Ellsworth, 1885, dentist; Will Ellsworth, 1885, druggist; W. E. Patterson, 1884, Real Estate and Teacher; S. A. Danford, 1884, County Superintendent and farmer; William Hurly, 1887, editor; S. M. Lockerby, 1883, attorney; J. H. Vail, 1884, attorney; J. E. Bishop, 1885, attorney; Z. O. Patten, 1885, farmer; James Walsh, 1885, attorney; C. C. Newman, 1885, attorney; L. L. Newman, farmer; H. L. VanOrnum, 1882, farmer; R. Wiper, 1885; E. W. Bowen, 1882, farmer and lawyer."[10]

Railroad History of Forman

At the time that Forman was first platted in 1883, it was thought that the Wadena Fergus Falls & Black Hills branch of the Northern Pacific would be built through Forman. Forman was on the line in the original survey of that railroad. There was also the possibility of the Milwaukee coming through Forman. It was soon realized in the spring of 1884, that neither of these railroads would be built through Forman. At this time there was a race for the County Seat and it was important to have a railroad to win the County Seat Campaign. To overcome this handicap, a company was organized called the Dakota Midland, with Mr. Becker of Ellendale as president. Stockholders and promoters in this company were Colonel Forman, R. Holding of Ransom City and others. This company secured a right of way from the farmers and had a survey made. However, they soon ran low on funds and in order to keep the right of way, they did some grading at intervals along the way.

After the County Seat Election in November 1884, the promotion of the Dakota Midland Railroad was at a standstill. Then in the spring of 1886, the Minneapolis & Pacific Company was organized in Minneapolis and they took over the right of way for the Dakota Midland. In the spring of 1887 the grade was completed through Forman to Oakes and in July the rails were laid. A depot was built in September 1887, in the east side addition.[11] When the railroad was built through Forman the towns people held a celebration. A barbecue was held with railroad men, citizens and people from the surrounding countryside present.

A celebration held when the Soo Line came into Forman.

Charles Krumm tells of a blizzard in January 1888 that blocked the tracks with snow. Only three trains were able to get through between January and April 1st. "At that time a snow plow came through and cleared the tracks." When the tracks were blocked it left the town without mail or food supplies. However, most people and

86 *Susan Mary Kudelka*

stores in those days kept a supply of food on hand in case the tracks were blocked.

For years all merchandise and mail was brought in on the train, with grain and cattle shipped out. The train was the only means of public transportation. Those people requiring hospitalization were also taken on the train to Minneapolis. Shoppers went to Oakes on the morning train and back on the evening train. Trips to the dentist were also made on the train.

Railroad agents over the years were: Charles Krumm the first agent, followed by Woodruff, Reginald Rickey, Martin Lund, L. C. Mann and Thomas Dougherty in 1911. There was also a need for a dray line, to move mail, merchandise and freight from the depot to its destination in town. "Some of the men who ran the dray line were Frank Argersinger, Clark Brooks, Olaf Enger, Pete Nockleby, Amos Grandin, Maurice Lae, Gene Hatch, Lloyd Bell, W.P. Smith, Lars Holen, Jim Scheller and Dale "Doc" Colby. Between trains they did work for people in town such as hauling coal, hauling water from the town well for cisterns or moving household goods for a new home."[12]

Grain Elevators

"The first grain business was operated by Andrew Land." The grain was stored in flat houses with wheelbarrows used to move the grain from place to place. Then there was the Osborne McMillan Co., which served the community for several years, and again Andrew Land acted as manager. Sigrud Anderson started another grain elevator. He bought the Perry elevator and moved it nine miles into Forman.

The Farmers' Co-op Elevator

"Five men met on March 9th, 1911 to take the initial steps to form the Farmers' Co-op Elevator. They were A.E. Land, N.H. Dyste, A.O. Dewey, F.A. Anderson and J.H. Bucher." "In July of the same year, the Atlantic Elevator was purchased for three thousand seven hundred dollars. This structure served the community until 1918 when a new elevator was built." "Managers of this elevator have been: N.J. Johnson, 1911; R.H. Jones, 1913;Charles Lindsy, 1918; and Earl N. Rice, 1919."[13]

The Farmer's Co-op Elevator was formed in 1911 through the efforts of A.E. Land, N.H. Dyste, A.O. Dewey, F.A. Anderson and J.H. Bucher.

Forman Newspapers

The first newspaper published in Forman was *The Forman Chronicle*. Mr. Johnson of Lisbon started the paper. Colonel Forman gave him a bonus of five hundred dollars to start a newspaper to aid in the county seat election of 1884. Frank J. Smith was in charge of the paper and the first issue appeared in the summer of 1884. *The Chronicle* was discontinued at the end of one year, that being the length of time Johnson was under contract to keep the paper alive.

In 1884, *The Item* from Dunbar was moved to Forman. Two young men from Lisbon, Alfred H. Ellsworth and Bob Doubleday started the paper in the fall of 1883. "They kept the paper alive during the winter of 1883 to 1884, although the town consisted of less than half a dozen houses." The newspaper was moved to Forman, because of the approach of the county seat campaign. The paper started in Forman just a few weeks after *The Chronicle* was started. *The Item* soon became one of the leading papers and continued publication until about 1894. In 1886, Doubleday returned to his home in New York and Alfred Ellsworth sold out to his father, Colonel D. F. Ellsworth. D. F. Ellsworth continued publishing the paper from 1887 to 1894, when it was discontinued. [14]

In 1894, Jay H. Maltby started *The Forman News*. Later, in 1888, William Hurly, uncle of W. C. Forman, started the *Sargent County Independent* at Forman.[15] William Hurly was editor through

Alf H. Ellsworth in 1885. He started *The Item* in Dunbar in 1883 which was moved to Forman in 1884.

Col. D.F. Ellsworth

1909. "Alex R. Wright, J.W. Wunn and E.M. Culver are mentioned as editors through 1911."[16] On October 20th, 1911 the two papers were consolidated. The paper was then known as the *Forman Independent News* and was edited by Jay H. Maltby.

The Forman News office.

In 1917, Jay Maltby sold his paper to the "Sargent County Farmers Publication Co., a local co-operative concern, organized at this time. Mr. Maltby went to Lisbon and took over the *Lisbon Free Press*. The Sargent County Farmers Publication Co. changed the name of the paper to *Sargent County News*." The first manager was Ed Vernon for two years, then Chas. Weston took his place. Later, E. W. Bowen ran the paper for a short time and in 1921 A. B. Johnson was hired.

Around the same time, in 1920, a group of local citizens started the Forman Publishing Company for political purposes. They started

Sargent County News office, Albert Johnson, editor.

publishing the *Independent Reporter* with Rollin Bronson as editor.[17]

There was also a paper started during the summer of 1908 called the *Sargent County Republican*. A few issues were printed, but by November the paper was a thing of the past.[18]

These various newspapers were housed in many different buildings. *The Item* occupied a building moved into town from Dunbar and located on Lot 10, Block 6. "*The Forman News* also occupied this building. *The Sargent County Independent* was started in the upper story of a building located on Lot 18, Block 7, which was also moved from Dunbar. After about two years it was moved into the shop on Lot 19, Block 7. This same building housed the *Forman Independent News* and later the *Sargent County News*." This building was torn down in 1929 and replaced by a brick building. "*The Independent Reporter* occupied one of the front rooms in the old court house, located on Lot 12, Block 11."[19]

Forman Becomes the County Seat in 1884

The County Seat was moved to Forman in 1884. The officers were housed on the second floor of the Groff Building. This building was located on the present day site of Martinsen's Hardware store. In 1888, they moved to a new building. The original courthouse was

The original courthouse in Forman.

The first jail in Forman, it was built of native boulders by Fred Kiefert.

located on the site of the present day City Hall. "In 1889, a vault for the safekeeping of records was built, sidewalks were added and a well was dug." In the 1880s a county jail was also built. It was made of native boulders and cement. It stood on the south side of the present day courtyard block. It was demolished in 1910 to make room for a new courthouse.

The new courthouse was dedicated on June 20th, 1911. An Old Settler's Day was held at the same time. The activities that day included, two baseball games played on a diamond on the present day fairgrounds. The Milnor and Havana teams played in the morning. In the afternoon, Forman and Cogswell played eleven innings, with

Forman winning three to two. Admission to the game was twenty-five cents a person and gate receipts were one thousand five hundred dollars. The county commissioners at the time the courthouse was erected were: John Sundquist, Peter Weber, Ed C. Enge, Nels Peterson and James Williamson.

Today, the courthouse is listed on the National Register of Historical Places. The old courthouse building was used as a cream station and a family dwelling, until it was torn down in 1947.[20]

The corner stone laying for the Sargent County Courthouse.

**Courthouse dedication in June, 1911
for people across the county.**

Old Settler's Day held on June 20th, 1911. A baseball game between Forman and Cogswell. Forman defeated Cogswell three to two in eleven innings.

Old Settler's Day in Forman, June 20th, 1911.

Old Settler's Day was held under the big top in June 1911 at the time of the dedication of the new courthouse.

The Forman Creamery

"In 1891, some of the local business men organized and built a creamery in Forman. The largest stockholders were John Dyste, N.H. Dyste, F. Mitchell and L. Steinke. The officers were: F. Mitchell, president, J.H. Dyste, secretary and treasurer and Mr. Norman, butter maker and manager."

"The object of this organization was to provide cash to the farmers for their milk. "In connection with this undertaking, Dyste Brothers obtained all the milk cows they could buy in the surrounding territory, which they in turn sold to individual farmers on a share plan. The farmer paid them half of all the milk sold until the cows were paid for. This plan worked out very satisfactory at first. Farmers could bring in their milk, for which they were paid in cash for the butterfat test. The milk was then separated and he could take back his skimmed milk for his own use in feeding hogs."

"The creamery made butter, which was shipped east. They made enough money so that all debts were paid off in a few years. "After about three years Mr. Norman resigned as butter maker and Mr. Miller was employed in his place." The creamery then operated for ten or twelve years, just about holding its own. During the summer months it made money and during the winter it lost. When "the cream separator came into more common use on the farm, business gradually fell off until it was found to be unprofitable so was discontinued in about 1907. The last butter maker employed was Oscar Langbecker. No dividends were ever declared and all money invested in stock was lost. After standing vacant for many years, the building burned down."[21] The creamery stood east of Highway 32 between present day Ekstrom's Repair and Todd and Jackie Ekstrom's home.

Dyste's Store

Nels Dyste started the first Dyste's Store in Forman in 1885. Groceries had to be hauled in from Milnor, as there was no railroad to Forman at that time.[22] Then in 1886, John Dyste built a store in Rutland. Mr. Silvernail and Gilbert Elkin clerked at the store in Rutland. During the fall of 1888 and the spring of 1889, Gilbert Elkin ran the Rutland store when John went back to Norway to visit his parents and find his wife, Mina Hoel. When poor crops were produced in 1889 and 1890 and the Soo Line came into Forman in 1887, the Dyste Brothers moved their Rutland stock to Forman. The building was also moved.

They began moving the building early one morning in March 1891. Ten teams of oxen and their drivers were used to move the building. "Among the drivers of the oxen teams were Peter Narum, Otto Anderson, Charlie Nelson, Ole Silseth, Even Dyste and John Stenvold." The building was moved on lumber, but as it was towed over the rough prairie the lumber began to give away. They then had to go to the reservation in South Dakota for timber. The building was moved northwest from Rutland over the old Indian trail. When they reached a big slough near the present day wild life refugee, a mile east of Forman on old Highway 11, a spring storm hit and they could go no further.

The building was placed at the rear of the Nels Dystes store, which is also the present day location of Dystes. Later Adolph Glovick built an addition to the north of Dystes store. He operated a furniture store there for several years. This building was eventually incorporated into the Dyste store. Among the clerks who worked at Dystes during the early years were: "Manley Jacobson, John Hurly, Robert Hurly, John Hohaus, Hjalmer Edmund and Harry Edmond."

**Dyste Bros. General Merchandise as it appeared
in 1908 with townsmen in front.**

History of Sargent County - Vol. 2 - 1880-1920   95

Left: Dyste ad from *The Forman News*, September 18th, 1908.

Right: Dyste Machinery Yards ad from *The Forman News*, October 9th, 1908.

Top: Even H. Dyste

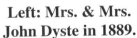

Left: Mrs. & Mrs. John Dyste in 1889.   Right: Nels Dyste

"In 1909, John bought Nels out and in 1912 John took his son, Harold into partnership. The store was then known as J.H. Dyste and Son."[23] Harold "served in World War I and shortly after his return took over management of the store."[24] "In 1914, the Dyste store hired the first lady clerk in the area. Her name was Ann Scoville."[25]

Banking

"In 1887, L. V. Babcock and J. D. Vail organized a bank in Forman."[26] A year later, in "1888, the Sargent County Banking Company was organized as a corporation and took over the two banks owned by David Vail and Associates." A few years later, in the "1890s, the Bank of Sargent County and Bank of Forman took out separate state charters. By 1895, business was a losing venture in Forman, the depositors were paid off" and the bank was closed until 1901. At that time Milnor then had the only bank in the county. At first Forman sent money to Minneapolis by rail and later to Lidgerwood.

In the late 1890s, John and Frank Mitchell organized the Forman State Bank. "In 1902, this bank became the First National Bank of Forman." Ray Himebaugh was cashier, he had been with the Milnor bank and was brother-in-law of Vail. In 1907, a new brick building was built. "A few years later, A.B. Carlson became assistant cashier and remained there until he organized a bank at Cogswell. Some years later, J.P. Gunderson was elected cashier and Himebaugh advanced to vice president, where he remained until 1924."[27]

The First National Bank was formed in 1902. A new brick building was erected in 1907.

A Farmer's State Bank was organized in 1912 or 1915. G. L. Strobeck of Cogswell, president, Ullen of Fergus Falls, Minnesota, W.E. Dada of Forman, vice president and Norman Cabanne organized it, cashier. In 1917, Mr. Cabanne left and Olaf Enger became cashier. The bank was reorganized in 1919 and W.E. Dada was elected president, Flittie, vice president and Anton Nelson, cashier, with N. H. Dyste, R. E. Hurly and A. B. Carlson as stockholders.[28] It was housed in a new modern building, which is today the racket ball building. This bank later closed in 1926.[29]

The Farmers State Bank

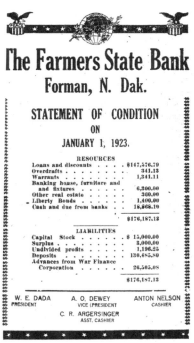

Right: An ad for the Farmers State Bank from January, 1923.

Hurly's Store

The Hurly Store building was moved from Dunbar to Forman in late January 1886. "A very wide path was made for the ten two horse teams and their drivers who had to walk behind them." Once they started moving the building, they could not stop or the sleigh would settle and stick in the snow. They moved the building on a bright twenty-degree day. "The store reached its destination without any mishaps." W. S. Hurly operated the Hurly Store with his two sons,

John and Robert. W. S. Hurly was also a newspaperman. The Hurly Store later became the Hurly Bros. John sold his interest to Robert and he managed the store for many years.[30] The Hurly Store was located south of the racket ball building, where present day Forman Fashions is located and in the empty lot next to it.

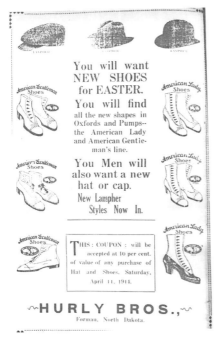

An ad for the Hurly Bros. store.

William and Ella Hurly

Saloons

One of the first establishments to be built in most towns was always the saloon and Forman was no different. George Haus & Co. built the first saloon, it was called the Silver Mine Saloon. J.C. Hill ran another saloon called the Golden Slipper. "It was written on December 31st, 1886, that Forman had two saloons and no water."

A year later, in 1887, Thune and Co. put in a lunch counter in their saloon, they offered "oysters, salmon, sardines and tripe, bologna and eggs." In addition in 1887, Langford erected a saloon. Frank Argersinger and Fagon also had a saloon that they moved in from Harlem. They called their saloon The Temperance Saloon.

Around the turn of the century, the W.C.T.U. or Women's Christian

Temperance Union worked to have saloons closed. They again became a strong force working for prohibition. "When Dakota Territory was divided, North Dakota came in as a dry state and saloons had to close their doors." However, people could still get alcohol at blind pigs. "These were places that still sold alcoholic beverages on the sly." Sometimes these were located in the back of a store or other places.[31]

Mosey's Store

This building was located south of the Sargent County Bank and was torn down in 1983 to make room for a bank addition. "Claus Evenson moved his store from Rutland in 1887 to this location on Forman's Main Street. Claus was an expert harness maker. He had his shop there until 1913 when he moved into Steimke's Hardware Store. Here he repaired and made harnesses for many years. The next owner was D.J. Jones who owned it for three years. In 1916, Carl Napravnik bought it and started his butcher shop. Later he stocked groceries in the front of his store."[32]

Steimke Hardware in 1886, Mr. Steimke on the extreme left. Mr. Steimke was the first licensed funeral director in North Dakota.

Right: The Louis Steimke home.
Left: Minnie and Louis Steimke, August 1899.

Hotels

One of the first hotels in Forman was on the east end of town and built by Mr. Wells at about the time the railroad came to town. Mr. Krumm, the first depot agent, lived in this hotel in 1887 when it burned, destroying all of his belongings. At about this same time, Sidney Mullen built the Washburn House on a lot west of the present day SEL Lumber Store. This hotel had many different operators and

The Washburn Hotel fire in 1914. The hotel was located on the lot west of the present SEL Lumberyard. Sidney Mullin built the hotel in the late 19th Century.

many different names. "Under the operation of Mr. Dewey it was called the Dewey House. Other proprietors were: Z. O. Patton, Mr. Peitz, Frank Argersinger, Mr. Manson, Mr. Otterson and Mr. Hoffman. This hotel burned down in 1914."

"The earliest of all recorded hotels were the Midland House and the Bellview. The Midland House was built by Colonel Forman and operated by his son-in-law, Mr. McDermott." Other operators were: Fred Richardson, Theodore Cookson, Wipers, Wells, Fergusons and Fred Groff. It was later torn down. This building was located south of the present day Martinsen Hardware Store. The Bellview building was moved in from Kindred and operated by Mr. Ewan in 1896. [33] The building was located on the site of the present day drug store. "It was originally owned by W.A. Ellsworth and operated by Scoville and Osten. In later years it was used as an office building, an apartment house and a restaurant. It was abolished to built the Forman Drug Store.[34]

Café's and Restaurants

Forman has had many restaurants and café's; one of the first places to serve meals was the Midland House. Edward Cookson bought the Midland House before the turn of the century and Mrs. Cookson did

The Midland House Hotel is believed to be the first hotel in Forman.

The kitchen of the Midland House. Mrs. Cookson at the stove, her helper is not identified, but may have been Mary Skroch.

Inside the Midland House, Mrs. Cookson is in the dark dress and an assistant presided over the dining room of the Midland House in the early years.

the cooking. Meals were served for twenty-five cents. The Wells and Bellview hotels also served meals. In addition, the saloons also served lunches at their counters. Mrs. Harry Forman also had a café on Main Street. In the 1920s, the Graf Hotel managed by Fred Graf served meals. It was a tradition to have Sunday dinner at this hotel and often times the Sunday guest list was published in the weekly paper.[35]

The Cookson Restaurant and Midland House Hotel run by Mrs. Edward Cookson about 1915. The sign reads, *A Good Meal, A Clean Bed.*

Livery

When farmers and other visitors came to town, they needed a place for their horses. "These barns provided a shelter to get the teams protected from the elements as well as provide hay, oats, and water. Some teams and rigs, buggies or surreys were on hand and available for anyone who did not have one of his own."

"The first livery stable in Forman was owned by Mr. Enstad. When his stable was completed, he invited everyone to a dance with

The Argersinger Livery built in 1888 by Sheriff Bartlett. The livery burned down in the mid 1920s.

lunch served at the Midland House." The dance orchestra was Wells, Happerstad and Graber. In 1888, Sheriff Bartlett built a large livery barn on Main Street. "The structure was thirty-four feet by one hundred feet and twenty feet high. This barn was later sold to Frank Argersinger who owned it for years. Sam Bell and sons eventually took over the management of the business and operated it until the popularity of automobiles. This livery burned in the mid 1920s."[36]

Telephone Service

The first telephone in Forman was in Dr. Bradley's house, prior to 1900. This is the present Kim Degenstein house. "Tax receipts for 1909 show that there was a Forman Telephone Company with receipts made out to W.W. Bradley. The 1910 receipts bear the name of Robert Hanna." Also in 1910, there was a Northwestern Telephone Company, which was thought to be a subsidiary of the Bell System. In 1919, Northwestern Bell bought out the others.

For several years, a tiny switchboard was located in the post office on Main Street. This building was located where the present day funeral home is. Frankie Marcellus, wife of the postmaster, operated the switchboard. The post office was closed at night and so no calls could be made at night. When a new bank was built on the site of the present day Sargent County Bank, the switchboard was moved to an upstairs room at the west end. Some of the first telephone operators

Early switchboard operators from left to right, Mary Bowen Petterson and Genevieve Bowen Keen.

were "Ann McPhail Scoville and Catherine Richels. Mary Bowen Peterson was chief operator for several years. Serving under her, either as relief operators or night operators were Genevieve Bowen Keen, Lola Argersinger Candor, Jonette Otteson Hansen, Irene Argersinger Skaarer, Helen Russel, Mabel Thompson Englerth, Archie Thompson, Margaret Smith Munson, Edna Dewey Taylor, Lillie Bowser Rowse, Charlie Dewey and Doris Stalter. Edna Dewey was the last operator before dial was installed."

For many years there was a line operating out of Rutland, which was thought to have been The Sargent Telephone Company. This was a stock company with Peter Narum as the head. "There was no switchboard in connection with this line. Dyste's Store was on the line also, so anyone in Forman wishing to visit with their Rutland friends used that phone, free of charge."

Another line was built in 1905 operating between Forman and Havana. This was built and owned by Henry Gardner, Andrew Land, Even Fjelstad and John Powers. "The patrons had to put down or set the poles on their land, then wire was strung for them. Andy Anderson and Ole Lunstad dug the holes for all the poles from the Great Northern track to Havana, receiving the handsome sum of ten cents a hole." There was neither switchboard nor operator so the patrons were charged only twelve dollars a year. When the line was hooked up to the Central in Forman, it was raised to twenty-five dollars a year. To connect Havana to Rutland, a switch was installed at the Jens Jensen farm. These lines were disconnected in 1935 or 1936.[37]

Mail Carriers

Nels Larson was the first official mail carrier out of Forman. He started on February 1st, 1908 and continued until his death in 1930. When he first started carrying mail he traveled by pony. Government regulation required him to carry a revolver while on route. He later delivered mail with a team of horses and a sled in the wintertime. During the winter, when roads were not in very good shape, he delivered to one part of the route one day and to the other the next. When cars came into use it became easier to make the entire route.[38]

Nels Larson, was the first official mail carrier, beginning in 1908 and continuing until 1930.

Lumberyards

Mr. Coy started a lumberyard in the early 1900s. This soon became Thompson Yards. As the town grew the yards were enlarged. "A large shed was built on the north end for coal. Railroad coal cars were backed in on a sidetrack and unloaded into the sheds. Since almost everyone used coal for heat at this time, this was a big part of their business."

In 1918, Andy Hvidston took over the yards. He is remembered for the beautiful flowers he grew in the window boxes on the front of the building. Other managers over the years were Judy Fangsrud, E. Holmquist, Charles Hinman, Ronald Olson and William Wright.[39]

Thompson Lumberyard

Garages

There were not many cars in Forman in the early 1900s. If cars needed repairs a blacksmith did the work. Charles Marcellus opened one of the first garages in 1914. Marcellus and Casper Smith built the garage. It was located on the lot south of Forman Repair.[40]

Churches

Congregational Church

A group of worshippers met at the Midland Hotel where they had services until it became too small, so they moved to the schoolhouse. "It was there in 1886 they organized with the help of Reverend Barnes and Reverend Griffith, as the Congregational Church. The following year negotiations with Reverend Stickney, head of the Congregational Churches of this region, were held to obtain a grant to build a new church building. A grant was received from the New York Building Society in the amount of five hundred dollars."

"Colonel Forman donated the land for the church building. Oxen and horses hauled a great deal of the material for building. Dedication services were held in 1888 for the first church in the community of Forman. Funds were donated for a bell and in 1890 one was installed. The company from which the bell was purchased even gave five dollars.

In June 1888, the first Ladies Aid was organized with Mrs. Groner as president. "They began a series of socials, bazaars and entertainment to raise money for the building fund." This organization was known as the Women's Fellowship and met once a month. Among the charter members were Mrs. Dora Argersinger and Ella B. Hurly.

"By 1897, the need for a parsonage was felt. A small building was purchased and again a five hundred dollar loan from the Church Building Society was granted." The parsonage was located on the present day Lutheran Church parsonage site.

"In 1907, a Young People's Society was founded under the leadership of Mrs. Erickson. Very good attendance and excellent meetings were reported." That same year, sidewalks were laid and two years later,

a light plant was installed.

"The ministers who have been ordained include: Steven Williams in 1896, Lewis Vaughn in 1901 and Arthur Seebart in 1920." The first permanent pastor was Reverend Mulholland in 1889.[41]

Congregational Church

Methodist Episcopal Church

"The Methodist-Episcopal Church of Forman was organized in 1885 by Reverend S.A. Danford, who was also a school teacher. The first meetings were held in a building west of Bishop's Grove," which was located west of Forman. "The grove was a tree claim of William Forman's and later sold to Mr. Bishop. When Reverend Danford was elected County School Superintendent he left the ministry to become an educator in the area."

"The next known minister was Reverend James Anderson who held services in the old courthouse. Reverend Gillespie assisted Reverend Anderson in a series of Revival meetings during 1892 to 1894. It was also during this time that the congregation became better organized. "They purchased a machine shed from J.S. Brandt. This was located on Main Street where Nelson's Laundromat and Car Wash now stand. They remodeled the building into a fine church in about 1895."

"The first deacons were A.M. Simpson, Geo. Hohaus, Robert Wiper, W.W. Bradley and A.M. Scoville. A short time later a parsonage was built. This house still stands across the street north of the courthouse and its known as the Ole Millerhagen house. Reverend Scott and family were the first ones to occupy the new parsonage."

"The Forman Methodists were often joined by other Methodists from Havana and Cogswell. Other ministers over the years were: Reverend Pringle, Reverend Mahon, Reverend Beer and Reverend McNamara."

In the early days, services were often held in the evenings. "Mr. and Mrs. Baker, Mr. and Mrs. Ray Himebaugh were in the first choir. Sadie Baker was the first organist, succeeded by Edith Hurly as early as 1897." Reverend Danford organized a Sunday school on April 26th, 1885. The Ladies Aid Society was also very active. The entire community and their families attended their meetings. They held picnics, which were often held in Bishop's Grove.

Methodist Church

By 1919, it "became increasingly difficult to find Methodist Ministers to serve the parish and the church closed. Most members transferred to the Congregational Church while some attended the Lutheran Church. Several years later the parsonage was sold. "The church building went, ironically, from machine shed, to church, to machine shed. The church building, for a time, became a repair garage and finally was torn down about 1923."[42]

Trinity Lutheran Church

The first Lutheran Church services were held in the Brandt schoolhouse, two and one-half miles south of Forman by Reverend Westerlund who was serving the Nordland congregation in Rutland.

On November 6th, 1887, a Lutheran congregation was organized. They adopted the name of the Scandinavian Evangelical Lutheran Church. "The proposed constitution was adopted and signed by twenty-one charter members: Niels Arntzen, Andrew H. Fenrow, H.J. Jorgenson, N.H. Dyste, Ole H. Reitan, J.C. Brandt, Peter J. Narum, C. Nielson, Henry O. Gardner, A.E. Land, August Lindberg, Edward Anderson, E. Fjelstad, Frank Lindberg, A. Sannes, E.H. Dyste, A. Sundlie, Martin Martinsen, Olaf Skaga, Ove Peter Christensen and Gilbert Even."

"The first officers elected were: trustees, Nels Dyste, J.C. Brandt, Even Fjelstad, Niels Arntzen, secretary and Even Dyste, treasurer."

Reverend Westerlund served the congregation until March 1891, when he was called to Horace. At this same time, the congregation also acquired its first cemetery. It was dedicated on November 4th, 1888 and located three miles south of Forman. "The land for the cemetery was a gift from Mr. August Lindberg."[43]

"The congregation was incorporated under the laws of North Dakota on January 8th, 1894.[44] Reverend Rasmus Lavik was installed on February 21st, 1891. He remained pastor until June 1912."[45] He held services alternately at the Brandt School and in Forman. Services in Forman were held in the Congregational Church or in the public schoolhouse.[46] Church services were held in the Brandt Schoolhouse until 1895 after which time, services were held in the Sannes Schoolhouse until 1906.

Reverend Gustav Westerlund and Mrs. Westerlund

As the congregation increased in number the need for a church was felt. "After due preliminary plans and resolutions, it was finally decided at a meeting on February 20th, 1906, that the church should be built on a tract of three acres, five miles south and three-fourths mile east of Forman, said land being an offer from Mr. Alfred Sannes."

Reverend and Mrs. Ramus A. Lavik

Money for the new church was raised by the Ladies Aid and by personal subscription of members. The total cost of the new church was three thousand seven hundred dollars.

The building committee members were Elling Jensen, John Lundstad and Peter Narum and contract for the building was given to Adolf Glorwick, assisted by Anders Roise. Later furniture was purchased and a Manelly Bell installed by the Young People's Society. President T.H. Dahl dedicated the church on June 2nd, 1907.

When membership in town increased, they felt a need for a resident pastor and more services, especially in the English language. It was decided to buy lots for a parsonage and church. "On behalf of the congregation, John H. Dyste bought the lots in 1911. A building committee had been elected in 1910 and consisted of Nels Dyste, Edward Anderson and Even Fjelstad. A parsonage and barn were erected in 1912. These building were built partly by volunteer labor and partly by subscription. The total cost of these two buildings was two thousand two hundred dollars. In addition during that same year, Reverend Tollefson was installed as pastor on June 28th.

Henry Gardner and Casper Smith as contractors constructed the church building in 1914. Funds for the church building were provided by the Ladies Aid, which had accumulated two thousand two hundred dollars. The rest of the money was raised by subscription and the balance floated by a loan of one thousand dollars. The Ladies Aid later paid off the loan. The final cost of the church was four thousand five hundred dollars. "Most of the furnishings and fixtures were individual donations. The church was used for the first time on Christmas Day 1914 and was dedicated by Prof. J.A. Aasgaard on June 20th, 1915."

Reverend I.D. Ylvisaker, president of the North Dakota District, installed Reverend Gjernes in Forman on August 12th, 1917. A graded Sunday school was started in October 1917. A Sunday school was first started in 1904 and taught in the Norse language for about five years and then discontinued for a number of years.[47]

The Trinity Lutheran Church Parsonage in 1912.

Trinity Lutheran Church, first used on Christmas Day in 1914.

St. Mary's Catholic Church

In the early 1880s, there were not very many Catholics in Forman. "The earliest record of a priest in this area was Father Hepperle who served Lidgerwood from 1881 to 1888. He traveled from his parish as far west as Oakes and Ellendale. Bishop Shanley occasionally came and offered mass. He was accompanied by his altar boys and a small choir. They often stayed at the Dougherty home in Forman. From 1888 to 1899 Father Dillon served all of Sargent County. Later priests Father Hanley, Father Barrette and Father O. Callaghn came from the Cogswell parish and offered mass in the old courthouse or the Woodmen Hall and often in homes."

"In 1913, Father McArdle of Cogswell with the assistance of Forman trustees, Charles Walloch and Thomas Dougherty, organized a financial drive for the construction of a church in Forman. In 1914, Kitterbush and Sons of Oakes completed St. Mary's Church at a cost of two thousand one hundred fifty-two dollars according to an old contract. "Father Hart, successor to Father McArdle, supervised the purchase of church furnishings. Various families donated church pews at twenty dollars each. Father Hart personally supervised the building of the altar in St. Paul and watched over it on the train ride home. Bishop O'Reilly dedicated St. Mary's Church in 1915. The first confirmation was held in the new church at this time."

"Charter members of St. Mary's were the families of Charles Walloch, Thomas Dougherty, Albert Frodette, Peter Lock, John Eiler, Joseph and John Fernbaugh, John Baltes, John Even, John Baumchen, Emil and Frank Glovik, Charles Rehak, Henry Nathe, Mrs. William Cookson, Mrs. J. Cookson, Mrs. Armstrong, Carl Napravnik, P.H. Murray, Joseph Kulzer, Matt Mahrer, Casper Nathe and Gerald Nathe."

St. Mary's Catholic Church

"Father Fogarty of Cogswell succeeded Father Hart. For the next few years, Forman became a mission of Cayuga with Father Stempl and Father Sullivan.

Forman Cemetery

In 1890, Lydia Gilborne, daughter of Colonel Forman, donated land to Forman for a cemetery. She donated twenty-seven acres of land, in the southwest corner of Section 1 in Forman Township. This was a portion of her homestead. "The first person to be buried in the cemetery was an eleven year old boy, the son of John Calvert. In 1889, a Captain Hilleborg was buried and Anders Anderson in 1891.[48]

Forman Schools

The first schoolhouse in Forman was built in 1884. It was a two-story frame building on land donated by Colonel Forman. Colonel

Forman also gave land for a small park, which was named Sidney Park in honor of Sidney Mullen, a thriving citizen. The park was used for many years. It was located where the Dave Jacobson home and bus garage are located today.[49] The school was on a block of land west of Lake Lithia. The first teacher was W. E. Patterson. The school had a very crude heating system, a homemade box cast-iron stove. "Some of the earliest teachers were: S. A. Dansford, a well known educator and Methodist minister; Mr. Simpson; Henry Ulve; Carrie Tisdell; Flora E. Baker; Nettie Herman; Canna Wiper Himebaugh; Grace Hohaus Wunn; J. W. (Will) Wunn, who also was superintendent from 1924 to 1926."

"In the early years much attention was given to eighth grade graduates because so few went on to high school. The first eighth-grade class in 1904 was Ida Hohaus, Helen Lyken, Meng Christian, Mary Groner, George Covey, Robert Hohaus, Harry Van Ornum, Morris Dyste, Grant Dietz, Lola Taylor, Blanche Groner and Myrtle Scoville. Henry Ulve was superintendent." The first high school class graduates were Percy Dyste, Albert Scoville, Grace Russel and Mary Bowen in 1913.

"In 1909, a new brick school was erected on the site of the old frame building. The old school was torn down and classes were held during 1908 in churches and the Woodmen Hall."[50] L.W. Holder, a contractor and builder, constructed the school. The school was brick and "contained six big rooms, besides a number of smaller recitation rooms, cloak apartments, halls, engine room and two large basement rooms." The school was dedicated in 1909, with a program arranged by Principal R.L. Rairdon.[51]

The first school in Forman.

History of Sargent County - Vol. 2 - 1880-1920   115

The Forman school in 1907 with Flora Baker, teacher.

The Forman school built in 1908.

The Forman school looking across Lake Lithia.

Flora E. Baker, Pioneer Educator

Mrs. Baker taught school for many years in Forman and in some cases taught two or more generations of families. She was born in Minneapolis on October 27th, 1868. Following her graduation from St Mary's Hall at Faribault, Minnesota, she came west. Upon reaching Dakota Territory, she taught a term of school at Milnor receiving twenty-seven dollars a month. After teaching for one term "she saved enough to buy a new dress, hat and shoes and get a ticket to Minneapolis to visit her mother." She later returned to Valley City and in the fall of 1889, she married Mr. William S. Baker and they settled in Forman. Mr. Baker passed away on January 26th, 1906 and Flora and her son, Clinton continued to make their home in Forman.

Flora E. Baker and Family

Mrs. Baker's first interest was in teaching, but she also took great pride in civic affairs. She organized Rush Chapter, Order of Eastern Star in Forman and was its first worthy matron, holding that office for five years. She also helped organize the Women's Literary Club, was active in the Red Cross and was a member of the Episcopal Church. She retired from active teaching after nineteen years and became Deputy County Superintendent of Schools in Sargent County for eight years and County Superintendent for eight years. In addition she served as director of the local school board for many years and did relief work in adult education.[52] Mrs. Baker met with a fatal accident in the fall of 1949.[53]

The Woodmen Hall

The hall was two stories and the second story was used for the Woodmen Lodge, Eastern Star and Masonic Lodge meetings. This hall was used for many things over the years. Before churches were built it was often used for church services. In the main room, dances, anniversary celebrations and other social events were held. During the era of silent films, weekly movies were held in the hall. Popular piano players played piano music during the movie. In addition basketball games were played in the hall, because there was no gym or auditorium in the Forman High School. Class plays and high school graduation exercises were also held in the hall. The stage was also used for declamation contests, spelling bees, Live Wire programs, Christmas Eve programs and gift giving by the community.

An important annual event was also held in the Woodmen Hall, a community Christmas Eve program. This was one of the biggest festivities held at that time. Early in the morning on December 24th, tables were set up along the west hall. The same ladies were always present to make things room smoothly. The ladies were: Canna Himebaugh, her sister, Elizabeth Hohaus, and Mrs. Jones, Mrs. Dewey, Mrs. Hurly and many other helpers. "Families in the town and surrounding area brought gifts for their families, relatives and friends in one of the biggest gift exchanges one could imagine."

The hall was decorated beautifully. A huge Christmas tree was set up on stage decorated with candles and tinsel. "Buckets of water

The Modern Woodmen of America building.

The Woodmen Hall, home of the Golden Fleece Lodge from 1911 to 1940.

stood nearby in case of fire from the candles." Many toys were placed under the tree and excitement ran high among the children. The school gave a program and all the children dressed in their holiday clothes. The school children performed songs, recitations and plays or skits.

After the program, Santa made his appearance. He carried a huge sack full of toys and candy. The gifts from under the tree were given out first. The high school girls passed out the gifts. Next, gifts from the long tables were distributed. No one in the hall was left without a gift and everyone went home happy. The Christmas program ended in the late 1920s or early 1930s.[54] The Woodmen Hall was located on the site of the present day tennis court.

Old Settler's Day

In the early days, a community celebration was held each year to honor the families who first settled in the county. This celebration was called Old Settler's Day. Over the years it was observed in various towns through out the county. The celebration included a banquet and program, which always included a prominent speaker. Throughout the day much story telling, reminiscing and fellowship went on between the guests. Often times in the afternoon, a ball game was played. In those days, nearly every town had a baseball team. In later years, most of the Old Settlers were gone, they either moved away or passed away and Old Settler's Day came to an end.[55]

Ice

In the days before modern refrigeration, ice blocks were used to keep iceboxes cool. Blocks of ice were cut from near by lakes and hauled into town or to farms for their icehouses. "The ice was packed in sawdust or flax, stored and kept until August or September." Most of the ice was cut from Silver Lake, Buffalo Lake and even Lake Lithia. "Many cut their own ice with saws and packed it in their icehouses." One store in town with a large icehouse was the Dyste's Store.[56]

Butcher Shops

Butcher Shops used to be located in every town. Meat could not be shipped in before refrigeration, so it was brought in by farmers and butchered. "The carcasses hung on a rack in the shop and were cut according to customer's order." At this time, the only refrigeration was an icebox. Locker plants were not available until the mid 1930s. "Some of the early butchers in Forman were Intlehouse, Starkey, Nels Larson, Carl Napravnik, John Lunstad and John Mosey."[57]

Doctors, Druggists and Dentists

Early doctors made house calls and trips to farms. Doctors used a team of horses and a buggy or sled to make house calls. They often had drivers so they could rest or sleep in between calls. Handcars were also sometimes used to get to houses near the railroad track. Doctors who have served this area are Dr. T.J. Halloran, Dr. Bradley, Dr. Ida Alex-ander, Dr. R.P. Wil-liams, Dr. C.I. Span-nare, Dr. H.B. Beeson, Dr. G.

The Dr. Bradley Home.

Warnshuis, Dr. R.W. Allen, Dr. Kenney, Dr. Aldrich and Dr. Robert Ray.

The first druggists in Forman were W.A. Ellsworth and Mr. Patterson. Later, Mr. Olson and Mr. Denk were druggists. Mr. Denk ran a drug store for many years. One thing that will be remembered about Mr. Denk is his dog, Deebs. Deebs was a German police dog that Mr. Denk purchased in Germany. He was a large, fierce dog. The dog only understood German and it was impossible to make friends with him. He was an excellent guard dog for the store. Mr. Otteson came after Mr. Denk and his family moved to Elgin, North

W.A. Ellsworth a druggist and operator of the City Drug in 1886.

James E. Ellsworth, the first dentist in Forman. He served the town from 1898 to 1949.

The town's first dentist was Dr. J.E. Ellsworth. He served the town for fifty-one years. His office and home were located on the present day site of the Price Funeral Home and the Forman Post Office.

Organizations

American Legion

"The American Legion was organized in Forman on November 8th, 1919, with Dr. Beeson as chairman. The following officers were elected: Dr. Beeson, post commander, Harold Dyste, vice post commander, Monroe Smith, adjutant, John Napravnik, finance officer,

Albert Scoville, Chaplin, George Merchant, Charlie Jackman, Otto Kastner, committee on bylaws. Other charter members included J.E. Davis, Olaf Nundahl, Iver Gronlund, Elmer Scoville, W.P. Smith, Lloyd Bell, Melfin Glorvick, Norman Holder, Albin Gronlund and Ben Moltz."

Legion Posts were usually named in honor of men who were killed in the service. However, since Forman was fortunate not to have lost any men in service, the post was named Sargent Post No. 82. Women also had a part in the service. In World War I, Lillian Carlson Gotberg was a Army nurse stationed at Salt Lake City, Utah. One man, John Napravnik served in both World War I and World War II.[58]

The first Legion Hall.

Eastern Star

"Rush Chapter No. 61 Order of Eastern Star of Forman was granted a charter on July 11th, 1908. Logan Chapter No. 2 of Oakes assisted in the organization and installation of the chapter." It was named Rush Chapter in honor of Mr. Rush. He was instrumental in organizing the master lodge and also the Eastern Star. The first officers were Mrs. Flora Baker, worthy matron, R.L. Himebaugh, worthy patron and Miss Edith Hurly, associate matron. "The first meeting place was over the Hurly Brothers' Store and they later moved to the upper floor of the Woodmen Hall. When the hall was demolished they moved back to the Hurly building, where they met for several years.[59]

Golden Fleece Lodge

On June 30th, 1888 the Grand Lodge of North Dakota divided into the Grand Lodge of North Dakota and South Dakota. At that time, there was but one lodge under dispensation in North Dakota, the Golden Fleece Lodge U-D in Forman. Mr. Rush, namesake of the Eastern Star in Forman, arrived in Forman in 1887 or 1888. On April 15th, 1889 the Golden Fleece Lodge applied to the Grand Lodge of Dakota Territory for a dispensation. This was the last dispensation granted. On March 9th, 1889, the Golden Fleece Lodge officers appeared before the Anchor Lodge at Milnor and were recommended by that lodge.

"Among the charter members were Benjamin Rush, George Montgomery, Amenzo, James Vail, William Hurly, George Merrifield, Albert Price, Edgar Hendricks, Louis Babcock, John Boner, Hamilton Emanuel, John Mulaoland, Thomas Nicholson, Charles Rust, Ambrose Willie, Cyrus War and Frank Zimmerly." E.W. Bowen was the first person initiated after the lodge was formed. "The first officers were Benjamin Rush, worshipful master, Lucius Babeck, senior warden and James Vail, junior warden." In the early 1900s they met over the Hurly building. Later from 1911 to 1940, they met over the Woodmen Hall. When the hall was torn down, they moved back to the Hurly building.[60]

Women's Literary Club

The thought of organizing a study club was discussed by Mrs. L.S. Taylor, Mrs. R.P. Irving, Mrs. S.A. Sweetman and others. Finally, Mrs. L.S. Taylor, put into action plans for a Women's Literary Club. "She gave a literary tea to which she invited Mary McCurry, Mary Irving, Minnie Taylor, Canna Himebaugh, Jennie Jones, Florence Christian and Louise Sweetman. During the progress of tea, which turned out to be a six-course dinner, there were literary toasts quotations and literary contests. A few days later, Mrs. Taylor and Mrs. Sweetman canvassed the town to find enough ladies who would start a study club. Charter members were the ones who attended the tea in 1884 and Flora E. Baker."

The club was federated in 1915. They also helped organize an

History of Sargent County - Vol. 2 - 1880-1920   123

auxiliary, which was called The Fortnightly Club, which later merged with the original. "The aim and intention of the club was to master everything written in the English language. With this aim in view they studied the English writers of the 14th century. They studied Chaucer's *Canterbury Tales*, Spencer's *Faery Queen* and much of Shakespeare, followed by Milton's *Paradise Lost*, Carlyle's *Sartor Resartas* and Bacon's essays. After finishing the English writers they studied the American authors, Washington, Irving, Cooper, Hawthorne, Lowell and others. They also used the Bay View Course studying Greece, the Renaissance art, Rome, Italy, Norway and Sweden."

"The study meetings were interspersed with social meetings, the principal one being guest evening, to which the husbands were invited." The club also formed committees for social betterment and civic improvement. "They showed movies for benefits, had war fund socials, gave donations to the Red Cross and to any of the local needy. They bought playground equipment, records and books for the school, a village flagpole and sponsored Boy Scouts. They met with the town board to get them to fill in and properly cover the slough opposite the present SEL Lumber Company. For years that slough was called The Ladies Slough."[61]

Butcher Shop Fire

Forman was lucky in the early years to have very few fires. However, one fire did occur in about 1914. The fire started after midnight and the church bells were rung to alarm the community. They woke up to realize that the butcher shop was on fire! The town's people came from all directions with buckets. A bucket brigade was formed from the fire to the town well.

"It has often been said a man named L.W. Holder arrived late. He had some dressing difficulties. It seems he dressed in the dark, grabbed his Long Johns and became confused in his haste. He put his legs through the arms and arms in the legs. He arrived late and somewhat handicapped in movement." Just about every citizen in town helped fight the fire in some way. One story relates, "Mrs. John Dyste, Sr., looked up and saw a man standing and simply watching the hectic procedure. She asked him, "Why aren't you helping?" He calmly replied, "I don't live here."[62]

Forman's Lake Lithia

Lake Lithia has always been a part of Forman. However, it was much bigger, before a large part of it was filled in. No true citizen of Forman would ever let it be called a slough. The lake does hold one mystery though. No one knows how the lake acquired its name.

In 1899, Joe Lewis built a wharf and boathouse on the east bank of the lake. Fishermen used the lake for years to launch their boats. When the schoolhouse was built near the lake, school children skated on the lake at noon and during recess. They also used the lake as a shortcut to school in the winter. After school and in the evening the lake was also full of skaters. Then in the spring, south winds would send waves over the bank and onto the sidewalk on the north side.[63]

Colonel C. H. Forman

In 1920, Colonel Forman suffered a paralytic stroke and was confined to his room at the home of his son, Harry. Up to the week before he suffered a stroke, he was full of mental vigor and enjoyed a visit from his relatives and friends to discuss public affairs and early events of the town and county. On July 15th, 1921 his friends arranged a festival in his honor, with band music and visiting and the Colonel was very much delighted. Then he suffered a second stroke, which rendered him speechless, and he lingered only a few days until he passed peacefully away.

The funeral was held Thursday, March 15th, at the Congregational church at two p.m., with services at the home at one o'clock. "The pallbearers were old-time friends of the Colonel, Lew Hohaus, Geo. Hohaus, Frank Argersinger, H. O. Gardner, O.B. Johnson and Nels Dyste. The school children marched in a body in the funeral cortege. Business was suspended through out the city during the services. The remains were laid to rest by the side of his wife in the Forman cemetery."[64]

Items from Newspapers

Bits and Pieces of Articles from
The Sargent County Teller

1887 - Intlehouse's meat market came into town on wheels from Harlem.

1888 - Arrangements have been completed for the opening of a race track south of town. Hiram Soule will be up from Taylor Township next week to survey the ground.

Articles from *The Item*

1888 - The work of grading Main Street is underway.

1888 - E.J. Barlow of Sprague Lake has bought Pete Intlehouse's meat market and will move to Forman with his family next week.

1892 - Adolf Glorvick, brother-in-law of Mrs. N.H. Dyste, to build furniture store north of Dyste Bros.

1895 - Burglars entered the store of Dyste Bros. at Forman last Saturday night and picked the till. They only secured ten dollars and there is no clue to the slicks.

1897 - David Lindberg died from injuries sustained in a blizzard.

1899 - The high water mark on gopher tails was reached this week when one of the kids brought in seven hundred thirty-five and received a county warrant for fourteen dollars and seventy cents, which he cashed without ceremony.

1900 - The Forman depot, which burned last Wednesday, caught fire from a defective flue. We will have our new depot completed by the first of May. An effort was made by the citizens to have the new depot built nearer the center of town, but the Soo officials have decided it shall be built on the site of the one recently burned – one mile from the center of the town. This means that the Soo people have great faith in Forman's future.

Other Items of Interest

Artesian Well dug 1904

"At a depth of eight hundred forty feet a fine artesian well has been secured at the livery stable and the water is as clear as crystal. Joe Hobbins is about to put down a similar well for Mr. Judson on the Belle Plane Ranch, half a mile south of town. The cost of these wells is for hundred fifty dollars – everything furnished."[65]

Team Falls in Elevator Pit

"From the back of an old post card written by Mrs. Marcellus to her son, Fred, at Columbia University, August 30th, 1916: "A team fell into the pit at the grain elevator this forenoon. It took an hour to get them out. They were only bruised a little. It was little Nels Dyste's team. Dick Jones' helper forgot to lock the scales beforehand."[66]

Jail Break 1920

"Four men in jail at Forman for a Cayuga burglary broke out. It was either a poor excuse of a jail or negligence on the part of the sheriff. Sheriff Flados is offering a fifty dollar reward for their apprehension."[67]

---

[1] History of the Town of Forman, Historical Data Project, from the State Historical Society, Bismarck, ND.

[2] History of the Town of Forman, from Bismarck.

[3] Century of Progress, Forman, ND 1884-1984, published by *The Teller*, 1984.

[4] Century of Progress book, 1984.

[5] History of the Town of Forman, from Bismarck.

[6] Col. C. H. Forman and friends establish town. Century of Progress book.

[7] History of the Town of Forman, from Bismarck.

[8] Colonel Forman searches for dream in Dakota, Forman Century of Progress book.

[9] Forman Flourishes in 1889, Century of Progress book.

[10] Forman's Diamond Jubilee History 1884-1959.

[11] Railroad History of Forman, Historical Data Project, from the State Historical Society, Bismarck.

[12] Century of Progress book.

[13] Century of Progress book.

[14] W. C. Forman Gives Pioneer Printing History of Forman, by Douglas C. McMurtrie

[15] History of Forman Newspapers, from the State Historical Society, Bismarck.

[16] Century of Progress book.

History of Sargent County - Vol. 2 - 1880-1920   127

[17] History of Forman Newspapers, from the State Historical Society, Bismarck.

[18] Century of Progress book.

[19] History of Forman Newspapers, from the State Historical Society, Bismarck.

[20] County government finds home in Forman, Century of Progress book.

[21] Forman Creamery, Historical Data Project, from the State Historical Society, Bismarck.

[22] Dystes Store, Century of Progress book.

[23] Dystes, from *The Teller Centennial Edition*, June 12th, 1985.

[24] Dyste Store claims longevity, by S.M. Thorfinnson, from *The Teller Centennial Edition*, June 12th, 1985.

[25] More on pioneer merchandising, by S.M. Thorfinnson, from *The Teller Centennial Edition,* June 12th, 1985.

[26] Forman Diamond Jubilee book.

[27] Century of Progress book.

[28] The Farmers State Bank, Historical Data Project, from the State Historical Society, Bismarck.

[29] Banking Comes to Forman With County Seat, Forman's Diamond Jubilee book.

[30] Hurly Store is moved from Dunbar by 20 horses, Century of Progress book.

[31] Century of Progress book.

[32] Mosey's Store, Century of Progress book.

[33] Forman Diamond Jubilee book.

[34] Hotels, restaurants help settlers get started, Century of Progress book.

[35] Hotels and Restaurants and Cafes, Drive-ins, Restaurants, from the Century of Progress book.

[36] Livery provides for transportation, Century of Progress book.

[37] Telephone Company, Century of Progress book.

[38] Mail Carriers, Century of Progress book.

[39] Lumberyards, Century of Progress.

[40] Garages, filling stations and repair shops, Century of Progress.

[41] Churches and Schools, Century of Progress.

[42] Church and Schools, Century of Progress.

[43] Trinity Lutheran Church 1887-1987 book.

[44] Churches and Schools, Century of Progress book.

[45] Trinity book 1887-1987.

[46] Churches and Schools, Century of Progress.

[47] Trinity book 1887-1987.

[48] Century of Progress.

[49] Forman Flourishes in 1889, Century of Progress.

[50] Churches and Schools, Century of Progress.

[51] School dedicated in 1909, Taken from the Sargent County News, 1909, Century of Progress book.

[52] Quarter Sections and Wide Horizons, volume 2, published by the North Dakota State Library, Bismarck, Richard J. Wolfert, State Librarian, 1978, pgs. 447-449. Original stories written by Angela Boleyn.

[53] Flora E. Baker, Pioneer Educator, Forman's Diamond Jubilee Book.

[54] Christmas program told, Century of Progress.

[55] Old Settler's Day honors pioneers, Century of Progress.

[56] Ice cut in winter keeps summer produce cool, Century of Progress.

[57] Butcher shops provide freshly cut meat, Century of Progress.

[58] American Legion, Century of Progress.

[59] Eastern Star, Century of Progress.

[60] Golden Fleece Lodge, Century of Progress.

[61] Women's Literary Club, Century of Progress.

[62] Bucket brigade battles fire in meat market, Century of Progress.

[63] Lake Lithia holds many memories and mysteries, Century of Progress.
[64] A History of Forman Township, by J.H. Dyste, Harry Forman, Flora E. Baker and Ella B. Hurly.
[65] From Years Gone By 1904, Forman's Diamond Jubilee book.
[66] Team Falls in Elevator Pit, Century of Progress.
[67] Items from Newspapers, from the Sargent County News, 1920, Century of Progress.

Main Street in 1887.

Young men from around Forman gather at the photo car at Perry in 1885. They are from left back row, Claus Evenson and Olaf Enger and from left seated, Adolph Glorvik, Hans Hall and John Dyste.

A bird's eye view of Forman in the early days.

Main Street in the early 1900s, looking north.

A panoramic view of Main Street taken on September 2nd, 1908. From left: barber shop, Ellsworth, pool hall, store, bank, Methodist Church, Leslie Building, which formerly housed the Forman News, next building a café, and last the Hurly Building.

The east side of Main Street about 1910, starting on the south and going north, the Sargent County Abstract, Dyste Store, vacant lot, Steimke Hardware, Drug Store, Printing Office and Newspaper run by Albert Johnson. The other buildings on the north end are unknown. Note the hitching posts on the south. The Sargent County Abstract now the present location of the Drug Store.

The west side of Main Street about 1910.

W.S. Hurly was among circus promoters with a parade of elephants through Forman at about the turn of the Century. Behind the elephants is Bellview House with apartments upstairs. Café's were later located in the building.

Walloch and Dyste, an early hardware store.

Feed Stable ad from *The Forman News*, September 11th, 1908.

William Forman, brother of Colonel Forman.

The E.W. Bowen home on the west side of Forman, later occupied by Keith Stalter, a grandson.

Above: A Forman post card.

Below: The Dewey Hotel.

Main Street in the 1920s, on the right side Walloch's Hardware and next the Midland House Hotel, the other buildings are not known.

Veterans in Forman: W.P. Smith, WWI; William Bowser, Civil War; L.F. Ellsworth, Spanish American War; Joe Lewis, Civil War and Jack Davis, WWI.

World War I soldiers and Forman veterans, in the background is the old Woodmen Hall. The men are facing the first Legion Hall.

CHAPTER 6

Gwinner

The village of Gwinner was "named after Artur von Gwinner, who was a large stockholder in the Northern Pacific Railroad in the early days. Artur von Gwinner was also a large stockholder and on the Boards of Directors of the German and the Spanish Banks. His grandfather and his father were mayors of Frankfort, Germany."

The village of Gwinner was created in 1900. "According to records in the Sargent County Office of the Register of Deeds, Gwinner was platted by a Mr. Almond and Marion L. White, who were husband and wife, of St. Paul, Minnesota. The plat was filed on August 8th, 1902."

"The Northern Pacific Railroad passed through Gwinner on its way to Oakes, North Dakota in 1900." The railroad had arrived in

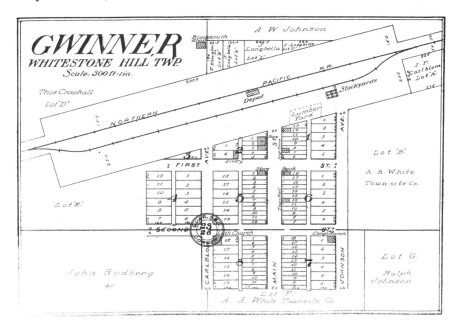

134 *Susan Mary Kudelka*

Milnor in 1883. A few years later, the railroad was within a few miles of Gwinner. However, due to financial reversals in 1883, most of the railroads in the county went broke. Then finally in 1900, funds were obtained and the railroad arrived in Gwinner.[1]

Some of the early settlers were Sander E. Lee, bank cashier, Frank Youngberg, merchant, Alex Mason, Sr., Feed and wood merchant, F. Safstrom, lumber yard operator, I.W. Meinhardt, blacksmith, A.N. Carlblom, general store, Nels Bjork, harness shop, Dr. R.P. Williams, Swan Friberg, carpenter, E.J. Hoel, grain elevator manager, Nicholls and J.P. Bearthune, drugstores, A. Korstad, restaurant, Reverend J. Edor Larson, Lutheran Church, Axel Johnson, carpenter, Gus Sandell, meat market, Erick Warn, barber, John Pearson, dray line, Fredolf Safstrom and John Ek, hardware, Mrs. A.N. Carlblom, first postmistress, William Lund, hotel and Lund Brothers, livery barn.[2]

Early Businesses

Gwinner Elevator

"During the course of its history, Gwinner has been the home of four elevators. Thorp Grain Company, a Minneapolis Line Company, was built shortly after 1900. The Andrews Grain Company was built at about this time also. Gwinner Farmer's Elevator organized in 1914 and is the only one still in existence. The Gwinner Farmers Grain Company was formed in 1920. It was later incorporated into the Gwinner Farmers Elevator."

The Gwinner Farmers Elevator was formed in June of 1914. "Several meetings were held from February to June of that year when Ernest Johnson and Otto Thompson decided to find out if the people in Gwinner and the surrounding area were interested in forming a Farmers Elevator. Ernest Johnson presided at the first meeting when they elected a Board of Directors. The first board members were J.L. Wicklund, Otto Thompson, E.K. Savre, W.M. Johnson and J.C. Silvernail."

"The charter members of the Gwinner Farmers Elevator were: E.K. Savre, Lisbon, J.C. Silvernail, Cogswell, W.M. Johnson, Lisbon,

History of Sargent County - Vol. 2 - 1880-1920   135

Otto H. Thompson, Milnor, D.S. Thompson, Orondo, Washington, Henry Nelson, Sherdain, Illinois, T.O. Thompson, Nevada, Iowa, Anders Nelson, Stirum, Edwin Nelson, Stirum, Henry Swanson, Stirum, Chas. M. Harold, Stirum, Nils Freeberg, Lisbon, Hilbert Anderson, Stirum, E.O. Johnson, Gwinner, A.W. Johnson, Milnor, Ernest Johnson, Milnor, Ivar Carlblom, Milnor, Anders G. Anderson, Stirum, J.L. Wicklund, Gwinner and Gust Holmgren, Lisbon."

"They purchased the Andrews Grain Company, which was on the site where the present elevator stands. The Atwood-Larson Commission Company was favored with the first account and E.J. Hoel served as a manager until May of 1917, when Ed Tunby was hired as manager. Mr. Tunby was called into the United States Army in August of 1918 and E.L. Miller was hired to replace him. Mr. Miller managed the elevator until June 1920, when N. Hennen was hired. Mr. Hennen was replaced as manager in March 1921, by George Lunneborg."[3]

Slaughter House

The Gwinner Slaughter House opened in the early 1900s. The slaughterhouse was located on the present day site of the Bobcat factory. It was owned by Gus Sandell who also operated a retail meat operation where the present J & M building is now located downtown."

"The slaughter house butchered, packed and shipped all kinds of meat. The shipping was done by rail. The cattle were driven into town in large herds. In the early days, the large cattle drives right through the middle of town were quite a sight." "The slaughter house was a victim of bad times and eventually was torn down."[4]

Livery Stable

"The livery stable was built by William and Oscar Lund and was just off Main Street in the northwest part of town. It was a busy place in the early 1900s." At the stable there were horses and rigs to rent. There are "records from 1906-1907, showing names of local people having rides to Forman for two dollars, to Lisbon for five dollars, to their farms for one dollar and fifty cents. The stable also boarded some animals, apparently for a short while, but it tells that feed was twenty cents or fifty cents."

The Lund Bros. Livery and Feed Stable in the early 1900s.

Dray Service

Gwinner, like most other towns, in the early days had a dray service. In those days everything came by train and had to be delivered from the depot to a place of business. "Records also show some feed ranging from one dollar to twelve dollars and fifty cents, depending on the size of the load, apparently."

"Some of the local dray people were Ernie and Kelly Pearson and Leo Anderson. They would meet the train and load their carts and deliver the merchandise to the proper business place. The carts had a platform, no sides, but rubber tires, so when they were loaded the men could push or pull them down the street to their destination."

Coal also had to be delivered to homes. "George and Bert Kjellin had horses and a wagon or sled and would load coal from the bins by the elevator. This they did with a shovel. They would deliver to the home and again, with a shovel, fill the homeowner's bin with coal for their winter fuel supply. There was hard coal, soft coal, lignite or briquettes and in later years, stoker coal, which was smaller in size. The variety that was used depended upon the stove or furnace in each home."[5]

Feed Mill

Alex Mason Sr. came to Gwinner in 1906 and established a feed mill and wood yard. He operated this business until 1925. "The wood was cut in cord lengths with a circle saw and sold for fuel."

Sandell Meat Market

"Gus and Olive Sandell moved to Gwinner in 1909 and established a meat market. Their home was on Main Street north of the Farmers State Bank building and their meat market was north of their home. All four of their children, Dyke, Perry, Gladys and George, were born in this house."

Gus also had a cattle buying business located in the railroad stockyards. It was located just north of the present day Bobcat office. Gus shipped cattle, hogs and sheep to the packing plants in South St. Paul. About 1920, Gus started his own meat packing plant, the Gwinner Packing Company. A fire in 1921 burned the entire plant to the ground.

"During the time Gus operated the meat market, he and Frank Youngberg, the grocer, installed an electrical generating plant in Gwinner. The wiring for the entire town was done by Dwayne Fuller

Sandell home and meat market. Those in the photo are Olive Sandell, Dyke and Perry in front of the house and Gus Sandell in front of the Sandell Meat Market.

of Dickinson, who lived with the Sandells during the process of getting the system in operation."⁶

Gus and Olive Sandell inside their meat market.

The Gwinner Packing Company, the company was started in 1920.

Kjellin Dairy

Emil Kjellin arrived in the Gwinner area in the fall of 1913. Emil and his family moved from "Langford, South Dakota with their horses, cattle, farm machinery and household goods. The trip took three to four days." In the spring of 1914, Mr. Kjellin started a dairy. Prior to this farmers had to separate their own milk and make their own butter.

"The Kjellin "kids", George, Bert and Allen, were delivery boys and delivered milk in tin buckets for five cents a quart. Later, a horse and buggy or a sled was used, when there was snow. Their dad soon had a Model T Ford. He put it in gear and let it slowly drive down the street, while he jumped out with bottles of milk and delivered them from house to house."[7]

Dahl's Store

Ole J. Dahl moved to Gwinner in 1919 and bought a store formerly owned by Mr. Intlehouse. Ole opened a general store. "He candled eggs, tested cream, sold groceries in the bulk, chicken feed with the floral sacks, Peter Weatherbird shoes, sewing materials, including thread and buttons. In the winter, they sold lutefisk and frozen herring and Christmas trees. Most farmers bought flour and sugar by the one hundred pound bags in the fall, so they were sure to be ready for the wintertime snow. Merchandise came to town by train and was delivered by a dray service to the store." The Dahl's also owned a store in Milnor. Their daughter Irene was manager, but she passed away in 1935 at the age of twenty-six.

"Ole J. Dahl was born in Granvin, Hardanger, Norway and immigrated to the United States in 1902". Before coming to Gwinner, he managed grain elevators in Buchanan, Englevale and Christine, North Dakota. "He married Anna Stubson of Christine on June 27th, 1908. They owned a grocery store there for five years. In 1919, they

Dahl's Store in 1919, the store is the center building in the photo.

The O.J. Dahl IGA Store.

moved to Gwinner with their five children: Irene, Joseph, Agnes, Lenore and Borghild.

"When the Dahl's arrived in Gwinner, it was thought to be a prosperous town. There were two banks, three elevators, a livery stable, taverns, pool hall, slaughter house, blacksmith shop, two lumberyards, hotel, meat market, auto garage, grade school, Lutheran and Congregational churches, newspaper, confectionery store, creamery and barber shop. There were also electric lights because there was a power plant in town. His family increased in size with the births of Kathryn, Orlando, Eugene and James. At one time or other, all took turns working in the store."[8]

Gwinner State Bank

"The Gwinner State Bank was certified by the state of North Dakota on April 26th, 1904, with a capital stock of ten thousand dollars. A.N. Carlblom was president and H.H. Berg was cashier. Sander E. Lee became cashier in 1907. The original bank building was a frame building. This building burned to the ground in 1911. A "new brick building was built at a cost of eight thousand five hundred dollars."

President of the bank, "A.N. Carlblom was killed in a train accident when the train he was a passenger on was blown off the track by a tornado near Foxhome, Minnesota. Mrs. Carlblom became the president in his place."[9]

Top: The First Gwinner State Bank, S.E. Lee is pictured in the doorway.

Middle: The Gwinner State Bank.

Bottom: Sander E. Lee inside the Gwinner State Bank in 1909.

School

"The first school was located near the present Mag or Dean Anderson farm. One of the teachers was a man by the name of H.O. Barlow, a most eccentric person. He was in the community many years, having farmed south of the city, also. The school was moved into town in approximately 1904, with Tillie Bjork being one of the first teachers."[10]

A new school was built in 1917 and was ready to be occupied in January 1918. Teachers at that time were, Professor C.G. Fisher, in charge of seventh, eighth and two high school grades, Miss Lauritson, the fourth, fifth and sixth grades and Mrs. A.G. Carlson as instructor of the primary department, consisting of the first, second and third grades. The building was two stories with a completed basement. The first floor contained four large rooms. The basement contained two bathrooms, two shower baths and a regulation gymnasium, fourteen feet high, twenty-two feet wide and sixty-two feet long, with a boiler room and storage rooms. The building was also wired throughout for electric lights. In addition, the building contained a teacher's room. The building was thirty-three feet high and cost approximately twenty-two thousand dollars. Heating and plumbing for the building amounted to around six thousand dollars. The contractors were Messers, Holder and Harris.[11]

The first school in Gwinner.

The Gwinner School.

Churches

Gustaf Adolf Lutheran Church

A meeting to select a committee to organize a congregation was held on June 23rd, 1897 at a school in Dunbar Township. A congregation was organized on July 10th, 1897 as the Independent Swedish Lutheran Church at Forsby. Forsby was an early town in Whitestone Hill Township located one mile southwest of present day Gwinner. This church later became the Gustaf Adolf Lutheran Church.

"The members of the first Board of Elders were Nels Bjork, John Ek, Albert Anderson, Gust Isackson and Nels Petterson with Peter Beckstrom as secretary." The first pastor was H. Sandell. He held services in the Forsby School. "On October 28th, 1898, it was agreed to build a church building and to have at least fifty per cent of the total cost of the building in cash before work was begun."

"Land for the church site was acquired by a quiet claim deed from the State School Board. The land was located in the northwest corner of the northwest ° of Section 36, Township, 132, Range 56." This land was purchased for twenty-two dollars and fifty cents.

"Charter members of the church were Mr. and Mrs. Nels Petterson, Alrik Johnson, John Ek, Peter Beckstrom, Carl Johnson, C.O.

144   *Susan Mary Kudelka*

Goranson, John Holmstrom, M.C. Vangerud, John Nickleson, Nels Bjork, C.M. Swenson, Oluf Melroe, Louis Halin, A.A. Wahlund, Adolf Sauners, John Johnson, F.A. Anderson, Anders Wahlund, C.G. Isakson, Henry O. Walstad, M. Bjork, Charlie Anderson, Carl Mattson, E. Gust Johnson, Elvin Lund, R.F. Goranson, Anders Larson, Oscar Lund, J.M. Lund, Magnus Anderson, Herder Anderson, August Anderson, Matt Wahlund, Eric Wahlund, A.J. Gabrielson, A. Swanson, Edward Isakson, M.H. Toftley, O.J. Gabrielson, and Jonas Sundquist."

"The building committee consisted of R.P. Johnson, Eric Backlund and Nels Bjork." One mason and one carpenter were hired and members of the congregation contributed all other labor. "Later Nels Bjork and Erik Backlund resigned from the building committee so John Ek and Frank Anderson took their place."

"On January 13th, 1899 the church was completed. The total cost of the church was eight hundred dollars. The membership was ninety-six persons over the age of twenty-one. The inside of the church was finished in 1905, with money from the Ladies Aid and Young People."

C.L.A. Blomberg served as pastor from January 28th, 1900 to 1903. He served as pastor every other Sunday. Miss Selma Wicklund was the first organist, one Sunday's collection being her salary. Next came Pastor H.M. Olson from Oakes. He served June 1903 to February 1904. Pastor John Safstrom came in February 1904 and served four years.

The congregation voted on December 1st, 1906, to move the church to Gwinner. The church was moved to Lots 17 and 18, Block 8. The church was moved in the winter of 1907 and 1908 using two steam engines. "In November of 1908, Seminarian C. Samuelson was asked to serve over the holidays and then was called to serve the congregation after his ordination in June 1909. He served from 1908 to 1912.

The congregation voted to join the Augustana Synod in March 1912. The official name of the church became Gustaf Adolf Lutheran Church and a new constitution was also adopted. "New officers elected were Nels P. Lund, August Anderson and John Holmstrom as deacons and trustees were Nels Petterson, Elvin Lund and F.A. Anderson."

Top: An unidentified group of men are moving the G.A. Lutheran Church into Gwinner from the country.

Middle: The G.A. Lutheran Church.

"Reverend J. Edor Larson served from 1912 to 1919. The first English sermon was preached by Reverend Larson and was so well received, it was decided to have one English sermon a month." Pastor Edwin Vickman came in 1919 and served until 1921.[12]

Inside the G.A. Lutheran Church.

Congregational Church

The Congregational Church was located on the former site of Philips 66 Station, which is today an empty lot. The lot is located south of the Over Time Bar. The church had "quite a large membership and a majority of the people living in Gwinner attended this church at one time."[13] One attraction of this church was the English language services rather then Swedish. The church also had an active Sunday school.[14]

The Congregational Church.

"According to one story, a Jardine evangelist came through town and was so eloquent that quite a few of the congregation left the Congregational Church and joined the Jardines." Whatever the reason was for the declining church attendance, there simply were too few people left to support the church. The congregation drifted away to other denominations.

"For some time the church was used for traveling evangelists to hold their services. Mag Anderson remembers the good acoustics in the church. He said that voices "used to ring bells."[15] The church eventually fell into disrepair and was torn down in August 1934.[16]

A Few More Interesting Facts About Gwinner

In 1911, the first major fire in Gwinner's history occurred. The Gwinner State Bank, a doctor's office and a drug store/confectionery store were destroyed. The Waloch Café is the present day site of the Gwinner State Bank.[17]

In the early days of Gwinner, the Rex Theater was a popular place. Silent movies were shown and young ladies played the piano for

History of Sargent County - Vol. 2 - 1880-1920

background music.[18]

"Records from 1916 show this as one of the wettest years ever. There was a severe windstorm, possibly a tornado and pipes were pulled from the ground on the Nels Petterson farm."[19]

In 1919, Nels Petterson of Gwinner was elected as a representative. He was later elected senator and served in the Legislature for many years.[20]

The Theodore Anderson Post 191 of the American Legion was organized in 1919 as the World War I veterans were returning from duty in the Armed Forces of the United States. The post disbanded in 1926 and members joined posts in neighboring towns."[21] The post was later reorganized after World War II

Gwinner, Sargent County, ND. –A Growing Village:
The Town is Fifteen Years Old and Has a Population 200—
All of Them Prosperous, Industrious, Happy,
From *The Fargo Forum and Daily Republican,* March 28th, 1916

"Gwinner, a small village of approximately 200 population, is located in the northern central part of Sargent County, fifty-one miles west of Wahpeton on the Fergus Falls-Oakes branch of the Northern Pacific railroad."

"The history of the village dates back some fifteen years in the time the Northern Pacific railway extended the branch from Milnor to Oakes. A. N. Carlblom well known, not only in the county, but also through the state, having held the office of state auditor, built the first general store, others followed and since then the village has grown slowly but in a steady, healthy manner, without any speculative dooms, so often disastrous to new towns."

"Of general stores there are three, two of which have been under the same management since they were started. There are two banking institutions –the Gwinner State bank, which is now located in a fine pressed brick building, has been in the business since the infancy of the village and the Farmers State Bank of a more recent date. There are two lumberyards, two hardware stores, a good hotel, butcher shop, harness shop, livery stable, farm implement house, barber shop, restaurant, drug store, feed mill and wood yard and one of the best equipped blacksmith shops in the entire state and three elevators, two of which handle coal, feed and flour."

"And last but not least, The Prairie Press, the local newspaper of which the entire community is justly proud."

"During the coming summer, there will be extensive building, besides several modern dwelling houses, there will, in all likelihood, be built a garage and a banking house for the Farmers State Bank."

"The residence section of the village is dotted with well-built roomy, modern homes. The people take great pride in keeping their houses well painted, a new coat of paint being applied at least every two years and the result is that the village, as a whole, gives a clean, pleasant impression."

"The present schoolhouse, having of late proven inadequate in accommodating the increasing number of children of school age, will be replaced by a larger and modern building in the near future. This new schoolhouse will be erected upon a plot recently secured for that purpose comprising a complete city block."

"The village has two churches. One is of the Congregational denomination of which Revered Mr. Haley of Forman is pastor. Of the other whose flock is affiliated with the Augustana Lutheran synod, Reverend Mr. Larson is pastor."

"A hall and opera house where traveling theatrical companies give their plays, a billiard parlor and bowling alley, constitute the chief source of amusement during the winter months."

"The country surrounding Gwinner is gently rolling with the exception of the Whitestone Hills from which the township takes its name to the north and west from the village. These hills if they could talk would be able to tell many thrilling tales of the time when Indians, buffalo and deer were the sole inhabitants of the country. On the crest of these hills many Indian graves have been found. The east side of the hills must have been ideal camping ground for the Indians and also a pleasant rendezvous for buffalo and deer, since there is a large natural spring located there, a haven for man and beast in a country where according to those who have lived here for the last thirty to forty years, drought was frequent."

History of Sargent County - Vol. 2 - 1880-1920   149

"The soil is a rich black loam from eighteen inches to two feet deep and under laid with yellow clay. Wheat, mostly that variety called durum, is extensively grown, though in later years since the variety called marquis has become known, this type had gained in favor. In the early years, very little thought was given to stock raising, but during the last few years this industry has grown to such proportions that from one to four carloads of stock is shipped out of the village from the surrounding country, every week during the entire year. Full blooded dairy stock, especially of the Guernsey, Jersey and Holstein type are found on almost every farm. The farmers tributary to Gwinner are right on the job when it comes to running their farms so as to derive the most profit from their work but they also realize that unless a little pleasure and some comfort can be had, when it can be had, profits from hard work are worthless. So they have built themselves good and in many instances thoroughly modern dwellings: good, large barns, silos and everything else that goes to make life more worth living. The time was in this community as in practically every other community in our entire land, when the farmer took his family to church or any other gathering he hitched up Tim and Bob to the only vehicle that could carry them all –the lumber wagon. Today it is different. Automobiles and especially Fords (God bless em) are as common today as were surreys ten years ago. And the farmers are welcome to them. They have earned them in the sweat of their brows and here is hoping that the people not only in and around Gwinner, but over this broad land will prosper in peace and plenty till "the last beam fadeth."

Some of the Business Men

"Gwinner has a large number of enterprising, up to date, hustling business men and all of them are optimists over the future of the town. Below we give a description of some of the business houses.

A. C. Carlblom, Merchandise

"Mr. Carlblom, the owner of a general merchandise store, has lived here for thirty-five years. When he first settled in this vicinity, there were very few white men to be found and he built the first building in Gwinner. For the past fifteen years, he has been in the general merchandise business and carries about a $10,000 stock of dry goods, clothing, groceries, etc. Mr. Carlblom also handles real estate and is an enthusiastic booster for Gwinner."

Farmers' State Bank

"This bank has a capitol of $15,000. It is strictly a farmer's bank and was opened last November. It is now having plans drawn for a $6,000 building, which will be erected early this spring. It will then have the best of accommodations for carrying on the banking business. The officers are: Curtin Cooper, president, A. E. Stevens, vice president, R. P. Johnson, second vice president, George Carlson, cashier. Mr. Carlson was formerly with the First National Bank in Milnor and came from there to serve as cashier of this bank. The latter reports a very good business."

George Sandback

"Mr. Sandback came to Gwinner in the year 1907. He was with the Farmers' Mill & Grain Co. for six years and then changed to the elevator company of which he is at the present time, manager. It is doing a good business and Mr. Sandback has shipped about fifty cars of grain this year. He also handles hard and soft coal."

Gwinner Farmers' Elevator Co.

"One of the businesses of the town in which a great deal of money changes hands is the elevator business. Under the able management of E. J. Hoel, who has lived in this community for the past ten years, the last two of which he has spent as manager of this firm, the farmers' organization has done a large business. E. K. Savre is president, O. H. Thompson, secretary and the directors are W. M. Johnson, A. N. Johnson and Ernest Johnson."

I. W. Intlehouse, Merchant

"Mr. Intlehouse is the proprietor of a fine little store, carrying a very complete stock of dry goods, groceries, boots, shoes, etc. He was formerly of Milnor, where he was engaged in a similar line of business. He is an enthusiastic booster and has a large number of patrons to whom he gives the best of service."

History of Sargent County - Vol. 2 - 1880-1920   151

Carlson's Peeriess Hardware Co.

"This company is under the able management of F. E. Hagedorn and is owned by H. E. Carlson. The latter came to Gwinner in 1915 and bought the business from the Milnor Lumber Co. of Minneapolis, in whose employ he had worked for a few years. The stock consists of hardware, machinery, fencing, harness, paints, oil, etc. In connection with its business, the firm handles Overland automobiles."

Farmers' Mill & Grain Co.

"Manager Theo. Odegard has been seven years in the grain business as buyer and manager of elevators. Few men have made a more signal success, both in increase of membership of his company and in profits, as well as paying top notch prices for grain at all times. The Farmers Mill & Grain Co. is the oldest grain company in Gwinner and always tries to give its patrons the best in the market. It has an up to date elevator and handles all kinds of ground feed. Mr. Odegard is a man who has the good will and respect of his fellow townsmen and he cordially invites the public to call at the mill whenever in Gwinner."

F. W. Youngberg, Merchant

"This store was established in 1902 and Mr. Youngberg has a stock in excess of $8,000. He entered the business field after making a success at farming, in which he had been engaged just outside of Gwinner. He has made a notable business success as a merchant, is a live booster and has the friendship of the entire community."

Stockstad's Hardware

"A very fine hardware store is to be found under the management of O. A. Stockstad and C. B. Bishop. They carry in stock hardware, cutlery, furniture, paints and oils, harness, gas engines, farm implements, lighting systems, cream separators, stoves and ranges. Mr. Stockstad also operates an implement business at Milnor, which he recently opened. He is an enterprising business man and has a large trade."

Gwinner State Bank

"Capital $20,000 surplus and profits, $3,500 tells the story of the

152   *Susan Mary Kudelka*

Gwinner State Bank. A. M. Carlblom is president, H. H. Berg, vice president, S. E. Lee, cashier and E. O. Johnson, assistant cashier. The cashier, Mr. Lee came to Gwinner nearly nine years ago to take charge of the bank, which had been established a few years previous. The concern owns a fine brick building, recently constructed and handles real estate, farm mortgages and insurance, as well as a general banking business. The officers enjoy the confidence of the people of the community and the institution is successful."

Thompson Yards Inc.

"Otto Hanson, the manager of the Thompson Yards, came to Gwinner in 1913, to take up the management of the local lumber yards, which were bought by that firm from the Wells Thompson Co. It carries a complete stock of lumber and building material and enjoys a very large trade in the town and surrounding country. It reports a very successful outlook for the coming year and Mr. Hanson is always willing to do everything possible to help boost the town."

New Gaiety Pool Hall

"I. P. Abrahamson, came to Gwinner in September 1915 from Wilmar, Minnesota and bought the Royal pool hall. He showed his faith in the future of the town by putting up a new building at a cost of $3,000 and adding to the equipment an up to date bowling alley. He handles soft drinks, cigars and candy and has an up to date place of business."

Kenoyer

"W. G. Kenoyer came to Gwinner from Milnor on March 13th and took charge of the hotel. He is getting it all renovated and overhauled and when the repairs are completed he will have an up to date hotel for the accommodation of the traveling public, as good as can be found in towns many times larger than Gwinner. He serves the best of meals and his beds are neat and clean."

J. Edor Larson

"Reverend Mr. Larson is pastor of the Swedish Lutheran Church and came to Gwinner in 1913, after graduating from the Augustana Theological seminary of Rock Island, Illinois. Besides his church at

Gwinner, he has congregations at the Oakes and Whitestone Hill churches. Reverend Mr. Larson may not be considered a business, but he is a busy man and is willing to give of his time and efforts to assist in bringing about a bigger and a better Gwinner."

---

[1] *Gwinner 1900-1975*
[2] Gwinner, North Dakota 1900-2000, *Gwinner Centennial 1900-2000,* 3-4.
[3] Gwinner Elevator, *Gwinner 1900-1975.*
[4] Gwinner Slaughter House, *Gwinner 1900-1975.*
[5] Livery Stable and Dray Service, *Gwinner 1900-2000,* 128-129.
[6] Sandell Meat Market, *Gwinner 1900-2000,* 131-32.
[7] Kjellin Dairy, *Gwinner 1900-2000,* 128.
[8] Dahl's Store, *Gwinner 1900-2000,* 124-125.
[9] Gwinner State Bank, *Gwinner 1900-2000,* 122.
[10] School, *Gwinner 1900-2000,* 21.
[11] School Building Completed, Article taken from the Prairie Press, January 10, 1918, Gwinner 1900-2000, 27-28.
[12] Gustaf Adolf Lutheran Church, *Gwinner 1900-2000,* 111-112
[13] Congregational Church, *Gwinner 1900-1975.*
[14] Congregational Church, *Gwinner 1900-2000,* 120.
[15] Congregational Church, *Gwinner 1900-1975.*
[16] Congregational Church, *Gwinner 1900-2000,* 120.
[17] Fires, *Gwinner 1900-2000,* 9.
[18] Entertainment, *Gwinner 1900-2000,* 11.
[19] Weather, *Gwinner 1900-2000,* 12.
[20] Politicians, *Gwinner 1900-2000,* 12.
[21] American Legion, *Gwinner 1900-2000,* 165.

F.W. Youngberg's General Store in 1900.

Main Street about 1900.

Main Street looking north.

The A.N. Carlblom Pioneer Store.

Gwinner in the early 1900s.

History of Sargent County - Vol. 2 - 1880-1920   155

Main Street looking south.

Main Street a little after 1900.

Youngberg Bros. ad from
The Forman News, December 23rd, 1904.

A.N. Carlblom

156   Susan Mary Kudelka

Ice skating on the Louis Halin farm between Gwinner and Cogswell in approximately 1905. Those in the picture are Ed Melroe, Oscar Melroe, Louie Halin, a hired man, Edwin Halin, Sig Melroe, Tillie Melroe Petterson and Ella Halin.

Middle: A dray line in Gwinner, pictured are C.A. Luther and Hazel (Hagedorn) Kempel.

Bottom: An early Gwinner post card.

The Farmers State Bank.

The Gwinner Garage.

The Gwinner Lumber Company and Friberg & Johnson Implements.

Top: Store of C.B. Hartwick and Co., general merchandise.

Middle: The interior of the Royal Lunch and Billiard Parlor, in January 1914, "Happy" Hagedorn at the far right.

A residential street in the 1920's. The A.N. Carblom home is in the foreground.

CHAPTER 7

Milnor

The history of the town of Milnor begins with the railroad and the town of Linton. "The Northern Pacific Railroad was the first to enter Sargent County, being built from Wahpeton to a point about three miles east of where the City of Milnor is now located, in the fall of 1882. The road was completed to this point but the grading had been done to within a quarter mile north of Milnor. This line was known as the Fergus Falls and Black Hills division and was expected to be extended to the Black Hills and on to the western

coast. Construction work was discontinued in the fall and no trains were run over this branch during the winter of 1882 to 1883, but in April 1883 a town was located at the end of the track on the southwest quarter of Section 1 of Township 132, Range 54. It was first called End of Track, then Graball and finally Linton after Nathan Linton, a merchant located there."

The first building erected in the town of Linton was The Price and Shuman Lumber office. "James Brown and Tim McLane established the first restaurant in a shack and employed Mrs. Graber as cook." There was no hotel in Linton. Travelers and new settlers slept on floors when the space could be found. There was neither church nor school but there were four saloons with the population numbering thirty, four of whom were women. The town site companies which platted the town sites at that time on the Northern Pacific extensions, could not make satisfactory arrangements with Severt Olson. He occupied the land on the south side of the track. The town site company wanted eighty acres of land along the north side of Olson's claim and joining the right of way, for a town site. So the Northern Pacific sent their surveyor to plat a town site near the center of Section 9, Township 132, Range 54 in what is now Milnor Township. "The railroad was extended to that location and the buildings at Linton were transported on wagons to the end of the line in August 1883. The town thus located and the township in which it was located, were named Milnor."[1]

When Milnor was founded in 1883, it was at that time the end of the track. A passenger and freight train service was supplied from Staples, Minnesota and Wahpeton, North Dakota.[2] Regular passenger train service began on May 18th, 1888.[3] "The passenger train was powered by steam locomotive, which pulled three cars, namely, a mail car, baggage car and a coach for the passengers."[4] A depot was built in September 1883 and was twenty-six by seventy feet. Upon completion, a grand ball was held. A telegraph line was completed into Milnor on November 2nd, 1883. At that time, Milnor had a roundhouse for its locomotive engines, a machine shop for repair work, a water tank and a section house for its track foreman.[5] In February 1895, the section house from Linton was moved to Milnor.[6]

Some of the early station agents were: John Ringstad, Henry Hauser, W. B. English and L. N. Larson. The tracks were kept up by section crews, with Pete Lee the section foreman. Workings under Mr. Lee were: Jacob Dahlen, Ed Bennett, Peter, Hanson and George Rodlund. Later his crew included Jacob Dahlen, Hans Dahlen, Hans Voge and Ed Hanson.[7] In September 1900, the railroad extension to Oakes was completed. Foley Brothers, contractors from Little Falls, Minnesota, did the work on the railroad.[8]

Early Businesses in Milnor

There was really no first place of business or home located in Milnor. Most of the buildings were moved from Linton immediately after the completion of the railroad to Milnor. The pioneer store owned by Nathan Linton was the first store in Milnor and was the first in Linton as well. "It was a frame building, twenty-five by thirty feet, one story high. Later the floor space doubled." Mr. Jens Pederson bought this building and continued the business until the fall of 1905 when the building burned. The ground was immediately cleared and a block cement building, fifty by sixty-six feet was constructed. More floor space was added later at the back of this building. It was always known as the Pioneer Store.

The N. Linton Pioneer Store.

Jens Pederson's Store and Milnor Hardware in 1906.

There were many early businesses and businessmen in Milnor. Here are a few businessmen and their professions. "Francis W. Vail came to Milnor in 1885 from Wisconsin." He was cashier of the Bank of Sargent County for many years, which was later named the Milnor National Bank. "While he served on many local boards, his highest political office was state senator from Sargent County."

"Jens Pederson, a native of Denmark immigrated to Minneapolis in 1873. He was a blacksmith by trade. He came to Milnor in 1889 and engaged in the blacksmith business. In 1892, he went into the farm machinery and implement business and later added general merchandise, after which he operated a grocery and dry goods store for many years in what is known as the Pioneer building. He held many public offices and was active in the affairs of the town."

The Jens Pederson Blacksmith Shop. It was originally built in Barney, ND and moved to Linton and then to Milnor. It was located on the back Lot 23 in Block 22, facing First Avenue. The building was later used as an ice house and a garage.

"Thomas V. Phelps came to Milnor in 1883 and operated a general store for many years. He was also in the cattle business and farmed to some extent. He was an accomplished musician with a wonderful voice and was much in demand at social functions and an inspiration to the Methodist church choir." He served on the Milnor school board for many years and was also the first postmaster in Milnor.

Dr. James McKenzie and Mrs. Margaret McKenzie

"Dr. James D. McKenzie, a Canadian by birth, came to Milnor in 1885. He was the family doctor of many of the old settlers. He was very active politically and was a member of the North Dakota constitutional convention in 1889. He was also the Milnor postmaster for several terms."

"Ole Hanson, a native of Norway, came to Dakota in 1882 and homesteaded in what is now Milnor Township. In 1885, he came to Milnor and engaged in blacksmithing for five years and then went into the hardware and machine business. He was successful in business and took an active interest in the affairs of community."

"Ole B. Jorgenson, a Norwegian by birth, came with his parents to Minnesota at the age of ten. He came to Milnor in 1885 and clerked in various stores. He later was head of the Jorgenson, Nelson and Austin general store for many years. He was especially interested in our schools and was president of the school board for several years."

"August Nelson came directly to Milnor from southern Sweden

Hanson Hardware Store and Moody's Blacksmith Shop, it was later owned by August Nelson.

in 1887. He worked at the blacksmith trade for various individuals until 1891 when he purchased the Moody shop adjoining the Hanson Hardware store. He operated this shop until 1916. He was a member of the school board for many years and took an active interest in community affairs."

"Henry K. Pennington, born in Maine, spent several years in Wisconsin and Minnesota before venturing further west. He came to Milnor in 1885 and opened a confectionery store, which he operated five years. He then entered the hardware and machine business as a partner of Ole Hanson. Ten years later he had his own store known as the H. K. Pennington & Co. Hardware. He also operated a farm in Milnor Township." "His wife, the former Miss Mary Wolfe, whom he married in Milnor in 1889, taught the first Sunday school in Sargent County."

"Dr. Henry W. Emanuel came to Milnor shortly after the town was organized. His trips to sick beds in the country on cold winter nights are a saga in itself. He came to Milnor from the east for his health and he evidently found it as he was noted for his toughness and it was needed on many occasions when the vehicle he was riding in got stuck in a snowdrift and he had to walk the rest of the way to administer to the sick. He lived out his life in Milnor. While his

History of Sargent County - Vol. 2 - 1880-1920

strong convictions and temperament made his enemies, possibly no man in Milnor had so many very close friends."

"James K. Taylor was one of the very early settlers of Milnor. He established what was known as the Milnor Lumber Company." The company sold lumber, building materials and also coal. "He sold out the lumberyard to Thompson Yards in 1915 and then built a garage, which he operated for several years. This building also housed Milnor's first electric light plant, with Mr. Taylor manager. Mr. Taylor served as police magistrate for many years."

"Dr. W. W. King came to Milnor at the turn of the century and at once took a great interest in the town and community. Here was another family doctor who was called out at all times of the day or night regardless of the weather. He interested himself in politics and was well informed of what was going on politically in both county and state. He had ability as a public speaker and was frequently called on to speak at local affairs."

"Ole S. Sem was a fixture in Milnor for over fifty years, coming to Milnor shortly after the town was organized. He practiced law and was successful in making money from the purchase of tax deeds."

"Other early businessmen who departed after a few years or were called by the grim reaper were Peter Intlehouse who came to Milnor in 1888 and opened a butcher shop, Anton Berger, merchant and later postmaster, Emanuel Harvey who ran a wood yard, Tom Harvey who ran a restaurant, Ole Gunderson who operated a shoe repair shop, Scott Wolfe who was in the insurance and real estate business and Mr. Nord who was in the jewelry business. A. M. Blythe, who was a schoolteacher by profession, operated a restaurant on lower Main Street for a number of years. Helgeson was an early merchant who moved after a few years, also Henry McNaulty, who was in the hardware business."

"A. E. Austin was one of the very early settlers. He clerked in stores until he went into the general store business for himself. He was also interested in farming. He held many public offices including that of mayor."

"Phil Dietzler, who farmed in Willey Township in the 1880s, moved to Milnor and operated a tailor shop for many years."

166   *Susan Mary Kudelka*

"Other later arrivals who will long be remembered are H. H. Berg who established the First National Bank, built the bank building and a large mercantile store building also a large house now the property of the Catholic Church and John Dakin who erected a large store building and operated the store for several years. Andrew Intlehouse started in business in Milnor as a young man and operated a general store and meat market and engaged in other business enterprises. Ole Stockstad was a hardware merchant, later in the garage business and was the town's undertaker for many years. A.W. Eastman was cashier of the First National Bank from the date of its beginning. Mr. Eastman was active in musical circles. His deep bass voice could always be heard in community singing."[9]

Additional Milnor Businessmen

There have been many businessmen in Milnor throughout the years. However, little information is given on these various businesses. Here is a brief description of some of them. N.D. Nelson was publisher of the *Sargent County Teller* from 1914 to 1942 and was also one of the first graduates of Milnor High School. "E.W. Wilson ran the Andrews Elevator in the early 1920s and later ran a restaurant. He was prominent in Milnor affairs." "Ted Macheel operated a jewelry and confectionery store, which was for many years the chief teenage hang out." Haldor Anderson, a talented artist who ran a photography shop for years, followed by his wife, Inga. S.C. Hoel was the city druggist for years and was well known throughout the county. Harry Reno came to town and took over his father-in-law's, Ernest Knapp's hardware store and operated it for several years. Later Harry started a Laundromat in the building." "Andrew and Olaus Intlehouse had butcher shops in several different locations through the years." "There were many carpenters in the area through the years. Two of the early ones were John Bengtson and Frank Engst. "In 1920, John Brennan, who had inherited the hotel from O'Connors, came to town to operate the business. John was a former actor and became a familiar figure in Milnor throughout the years. He operated the hotel until it burned in 1934. After the fire, he returned to Hollywood and his former profession." Milnor also had many doctors over the years. Later medical doctors were George Mitchell, Dr. Veitch, Dr. Campbell and J. E. Witters.[10]

Milnor City Government

Milnor was created in the summer of 1883 when the railroad from Linton reached the present day site of Milnor. The buildings were moved from Linton and Milnor was established. "A petition was filed with the County Commissioners of Sargent County, Dakota Territory, that Milnor, Dakota Territory, be incorporated into the town of Milnor in 1884. There were one hundred and two signatures on the petition. The plat of Milnor, Dakota Territory as surveyed by J. H. Herring was Section 9, Township 132, Range 54." The total land area was 588 3/5 acres and if Storm Lake was included it was six hundred and forty acres. The total population of Milnor at that time was two hundred fifty-two and the number of voters was one hundred and nine. "The petition was granted. The election to incorporate was held on June 30th, 1884, at which time forty-seven voted for and thirty-four against."

Milnor officially became a town on July 8th, 1884. The election for town officers was on July 21st, 1884. However, a record of these officers in not available. A few of the civil achievements in the early days of Milnor was the building of the jail in 1884, sidewalks laid in 1904 and street lighting put in place in the early 1900s.[11] Milnor became a city in 1914, with L.W. Intlehouse as the first mayor.[12]

Sargent County Teller

The Sargent County Teller was established at Linton and Mr. Fred Falley printed the first issue May 19th, 1883. Mr. Falley soon moved his office to Milnor. Once in Milnor, "Mr. George Fritz entered into partnership with Mr. Falley and they erected a building." *The Teller* was printed in the front of the building and the two young men and

The first home of *The Sargent County Teller*.

An early photo of *The Teller*.

their wives occupied the rooms on the second floor. "Mr. Falley was sergeant-at-arms during the constitutional convention at Bismarck in 1889 and served as secretary of state in North Dakota from 1897 to 1900." Later, Mrs. D. E. Allen occupied the building for twenty years where she operated a boarding house.[13]

Post Office

The post office was established in October 1883. "An application for the establishment of a post office was sent to the Postmaster General of the United States on July 31st, 1883 by Albert F. Price, then of Linton. At this time the residents of Linton received their mail at the Sydna post office, which was located in the home of James C. Lanegan, (three miles northwest of Milnor). Sydna post office was located on the mail route from Lisbon to Hamlin, the mail carrier at that time being W. R. Stoddard. In answer to routine question on the application blank, it was established that mail would be supplied from Wahpeton instead of Lisbon as soon as regular train service into Milnor was established."

"The first postmaster was Thomas V. Phelps, who received his appointment October 18th, 1883, at which time a post office was established at Milnor. Names of the postmasters and dates of their appointments were: Thomas V. Phelps, 1883; Charles B. Stowe, 1885;

Elmer Willey, 1887; James D. McKenzie, 1889; Theodore Johnson, 1893; Elmer Willey, 1893; John T. McNulty, 1896; Jay H. Maltby, 1897; James D. McKenzie, 1900; Anton Berger, 1909; J. G. Boatman, 1913 to 1926."

"Mail routes were established to supply the various outlying districts. Some of these early routes were: Milnor to Ellendale (1884), Milnor to Ransom City, and Milnor to Forman. The post office has been located in many different buildings since it was established. The first was in the store of Thomas V. Phelps." Vail Security Company erected the next building in 1918. This building was a bank first and then a post office. Today this building is located next to Shoes and Stuff and is used by J & M Printing.

Rural free delivery service was established early in 1900. At first there were four routes, which were later combined into two after the use of cars instead of the horses and mail wagons. "Some of the early mail carriers were Henry Elliott, James A. Payne, John Stockstad, Nick Sterno and W. Edwards."[14]

Milnor mail carriers about 1912.

The Call House

The Call House was built in the late summer and fall of 1883. It was located on the north side of the railroad track. "Meals were served in a tent until the building was completed." This hotel was later converted into a creamery. When the creamery was closed, Mr. Jens Pedersen bought the building, had it moved to the west side of town and used it as a barn and garage.[15]

Jail

A jail was built in 1884. It was a one-cell structure with a small room for an attendant and was in use until the middle 1930s. It was never occupied frequently, or ever overcrowded.[16]

The Call House.

The Milnor Fire Department

The Milnor Fire Department was organized some time before 1900. The actual date of organization is not known. Around 1900, two chemical units were purchased. These units were housed in the fire hall and pulled by horses. Crews manned the units with each man trained to handle his own position. These two units were used for many years.[17]

An early jail in Milnor.

Standard Oil Bulk Station

"The first Standard Bulk Plant was installed in Milnor in about 1902. At that time Louis Larson took the job as agent.

Milnor Rural Telephone

Frank Vail formed the Milnor Rural Telephone Company about 1910. Offices were originally located above the building known as the Pioneer Store.[18]

History of Sargent County - Vol. 2 - 1880-1920   171

Farmers Grain & Trading Company

"Farmers Grain and Trading Company began business in March of 1913. The first board of directors were: D.A. Cross, Ed Enge, H.P. Holt, George Flamer, A.A. Stockstad and H.P. Marquette. The manager they chose was H.E. Wyum. During the first year of business, they leased a facility handling mainly flour and coal for its patrons. The new facility was built in the spring of 1914 and is still in use."[19]

Thompson Yards

"Thompson Yards bought the Taylor lumberyard in 1915. It was located across from the present site of the bus barn". A stone building located on Third Street was there office. "The yards on Main Street were built starting in 1917 and continued in business until they closed in the fall of 1958."[20]

Pharmacy

S. Hoel operated a pharmacy in the building, which is now Milnor Clothing. "S. Hoel originally started a pharmacy about 1916; however, his first pharmacy was not in this building, but in a building at a different location on this street.[21]

Milnor Co-operative Creamery & Produce Association

"The Milnor Co-operative Creamery was the first co-operative in the state of North Dakota." A Board of directors meeting was held on November 3rd, 1917 and the following were appointed to the board, Logan Stanley, President; J. Tanner, Vice President; H. A. Rothhouse, Secretary; H. P. Holt, Treasurer; Directors: E. J. Ryan, Henry Brissman, Price Boatman, P.A. Stranberg."

The creamery and icehouse was located on the east side of the street on the first four lots closest to the Farmers Grain & Trading Company Elevator. The creamery paid one hundred dollars for the four lots. The first annual stockholders' meeting was on January 14th, 1918 at Milnor High School. At the meeting, by-laws were adopted and an application for charter was made. "The directors were instructed not to exceed six thousand dollars in building and equipping the creamery."

The Milnor Cooperative Creamery.

"It was decided to build the creamery thirty-six by forty-four feet by eleven and a half feet high. They purchased creamery equipment at New Effington, South Dakota for six hundred dollars." To celebrate the opening of the creamery, a picnic was held June 29th, 1918. In 1920, the creamery was not making enough to care for its expenses, so a special meeting was held. At the meeting it was decided to sell stock to anyone, whether they owned milk or not.

"In January 1919, John Gersch filled the ice house with two hundred tons of ice packed with sawdust for three hundred dollars. Later that year in April, "the price was seven cents a quart for sweet milk delivered to the creamery for ice cream purposes." The creamery made ice cream on order for patrons of the creamery, orders in by Thursday were made on Saturday." "In 1919, they ordered one hundred twenty-five tons of ice from Battle Lake at one dollar a ton. In 1920, the Farmer's Creamery closed and opened again in 1921."[22]

Milnor Theatre

Bill Nordstrom built the Iris Theatre in 1917. Bill ran the theater until 1933 when he lost it to E.B. Johnson who sold it to Nels Nelson.[23]

The Iris Theatre, the first theatre in Milnor.

History of Sargent County - Vol. 2 - 1880-1920   173

John Edison's Service Shop

"John Edison started an auto shop in Milnor in 1918. "John was born in Sweden in 1895, immigrated to the United States in 1912 at the age of seventeen and came to New York Mills, Minnesota to an uncle's." After completing a course in auto mechanics and driving in Minneapolis, he operated an auto shop in Minneapolis. He then returned to New York Mills to work as an auto mechanic for several Ford dealerships."

"In 1918, John came to Milnor and opened a tire repair and service shop. When the United States became involved in World War I, John enlisted. "In 1919, John returned to New York Mills, married Maggie Sturdevant and returned to Milnor, re-entering the auto service business in his former spot. In 1920, John moved his garage to the J.K. Taylor building and was there until 1925." [24]

Merchandise and Hardware

In the early days of Milnor, there were many stores. Here are a few. N. Linton, A.P. Williams, Halgorson, Hanson and Phelps all had stores, with well kept stocks. "Riddle and Eastman were hardware merchants. R.L. Falley kept a drugstore and practiced medicine. R. Jeanson had a furniture store. Price and Shuman, Bartlett and Wolfe, Riddle and Eastman were lumber dealers. Bartlett and Wolfe and H. Thompson and Co. sold machinery. Real estate firms were those of Berg and Bishop, P.M. Chandler, J.A. Walsh, W.J. Hughes, C.C. Newman and J.H. Vail. Palmer and Brown sold wood and R. Jeanson sold coal and fuel." Two early hotels in Milnor were the Runkle House and the Winston House. "Sam Palmer maintained a fine livery stable." Rice Buley, Neygaard, Hendrickson and H. Thompson ran early saloons in town.[25]

Banking History

Mr. F.W. Vail came to Milnor on November 2nd, 1885. Mr. Vail was to run The Bank of Sargent County, a private institution owned by J.E. Bishop and bought by David F. Vail. This was the first bank in Sargent County. For six months previous, Mr. F.W. Vail had been training in the banking business of Dakota with the firm of White &

Kellogg who opened the Northwestern Bank in Wahpeton, North Dakota."

J.E. Bishop and some Fargo associates established the Bank of Sargent County in Milnor in late 1883 or early 1884. "Mrs. Bishop was acting as cashier in the bank at the time." The bank was "operated as a private bank until 1887, when owing to the removal of the County Seat from Milnor to Forman, the Bank of Forman was also established with L.V. Babcock in charge and J.D. Vail assistant cashier. In 1888, the Sargent County Banking Company was organized as a corporation taking over the two banks owned by D.F. Vail and associates."

"These banks were continued in that way until the passage of a state bank law in the early 1890s, at which time the Bank of Sargent County and the Bank of Forman took out separate charters. Things ran smoothly until 1893 when a panic came and a period of deflation arrived which continued through 1896 and 1897. In 1895, finding the business was a losing venture at Forman they paid off the depositors and closed the bank." Mr. Babcock was then employed with "St. Paul Fire and Marine Insurance Company as special agent and adjuster, continuing in its service until his death in 1908. J.D. Vail also went into the insurance business for Hartford Fire Insurance Company as assistant general agent in the central department at Chicago."

"The Bank of Sargent County at Milnor was the only bank in Sargent County for a time after closing the bank at Forman." However, it did not take long for more banks to open. "In 1901, prosperity again came to the county and banks were opened over the next few years in Cogswell, Forman, Havana, Rutland, Cayuga, Geneseo, DeLamere, Gwin-

The Bank of Sargent County is at the left and the Milnor National Bank, the successor of the Bank of Sargent County is on the right.

History of Sargent County - Vol. 2 - 1880-1920 **175**

ner, Stirum and Crete." These towns all had one or more banks.

"In 1906, the First National Bank of Milnor was organized, whereupon the Bank of Sargent County was converted into a National Banking Institution."[26] The bank opened for business on September 14th, 1906. James McGann was elected temporary president and A.W. Eastman as secretary. The first stockholder meeting was on January 1st, 1907 and the following directors were elected: A.W. Eastman, H.H. Berg, O.B. Jorgenson, O.S. Sem, Hans Johnson, H.C. Johnson, W.L. Carter, Joseph Patterson and D.J. Jones.[27] "There was no change in the management and it remained with David F. Vail as its president until his death in 1908."[28]

The Milnor School

The board of County Commissioners defined the school district boundaries on November 2nd, 1883. "District number two, which was the Milnor school district consisted of Township 132, Range 54 and the east half of Township 132, Range 55. The election for the school officers was held on the 24th day of November 1883. Officers elected were: A. P. Williams, president, Samuel Palmer, director and Theodore Johnson, clerk. The district was named Milnor." Mrs. Nancy G. Herring was Superintendent of Schools in Sargent County at the time. She had also been elected in November.

The first school in Milnor was erected in 1884, on the north side of the Northern Pacific Railroad tracks. "It was a two-story frame structure of four rooms, heated with stoves." It was completed in November and a grand ball celebrated that event before the furniture was installed. "It was a great occasion, this celebrating the completion of the first town school building in the county."

When the new school opened, the number of school age residents was eighty-seven. The first teacher was Lewis Camfield. By 1886, the school had grown and two teachers were employed, Miss Emma Bates as principal and Mary Wolfe (later she became Mrs. H. K. Pennington) of Milnor as assistant in charge of the lower grades.

In 1894, the school building was moved to the site of the present day school. At that time, the school children planted cottonwood trees, which grew, around the school grounds for many years. A few

The first Milnor School.

Milnor School

years earlier, in 1888, the first teacher's institute in what is now Sargent County was also held in this school. Milnor High School's first graduating class was the class of 1900. The graduates finished a three-year course. The class consisted of Axel Nelson and Hannah Lavik. In 1904, the building was destroyed by fire from an overheated furnace and all school records were destroyed. The school board immediately made arrangements for school to be held in the churches until a new building could be constructed. Later that same year a new building was completed. The new school was made of brick and had four rooms and a playroom in the basement. Later the basement was used as a domestic science room. When the new school was built four teachers were employed and a few high school subjects were given.

In 1914, an addition was made to the school. The schoolhouse was considered too large and the high school assembly room was to be used as a community center. However, in a few years the school needed the space for a high school assembly and study room. During the 1914 to 1915 school year, the school became a second-class high school. A few years later, in 1917 the rural schools of Milnor Township were consolidated with the city of Milnor.[29]

Territorial Normal School

Milnor had a Territorial Normal School from 1887 to 1889. The school was held in the Milnor school building, which was at that time located on the north side of the railroad tracks. The school was partly supported by the Territory of Dakota but largely by local subscription.[30] Professor John Ogden was principal of the school, F. W. Vail secretary of the board of education, John Walsh a local attorney was president and there were five assistant teachers.[31] "John Ogden was born in Ohio and educated there and in Delaware. He came to North Dakota in 1887 to file on a homestead."[32] Mr. Ogden was also Superintendent of Public Instruction in North Dakota from 1891 to 1902.

The women of Milnor organized a sort of auxiliary to care for the welfare of the out of town students. The auxiliary with some of the men folk hired the Milnor

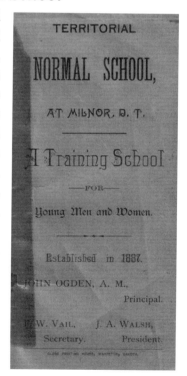

Territorial Normal School at Milnor pamphlet.

Hotel owned and run by Matt Miner. The townspeople gathered together odd pieces of furniture and established a dormitory in the hotel where the students could eat and sleep. "One of the teachers was given a room in return for acting as housemother. Certain rules and regulations were evolved so as to make it nearly self-sustaining. Outside students brought supplies such as bread, potatoes and meat from the country and the student body managed to get funds to buy groceries.

Some of the students were: Flora Rice, who became Mrs. Flora Baker, Sargent County's Superintendent; Ella Brown from Minnewauken, who became Mrs. J.A.G. Risk, Lisbon, North Dakota; Kate Tarault, Minnewauken, who married Fred Snore, a pioneer of Benson County; Ethleen Knuppenburg, who came from Richland County, she married W.L. Williamson; Mary Wolfe, who married Henry Pennington; Ole Sem, a lawyer, Milnor and Andrew Intlehouse, leader of the First Regiment Band at Lisbon.[33]

Churches

Presbyterian Church

Presbyterian Church

"The Milnor Presbyterian Church was the first one built in Sargent County. A congregational meeting was held in the Mills Building on May 13th, 1884, for the purpose of taking the necessary steps to organize a Presbyterian Church at Milnor, Dakota Territory Reverend F.M. Wood, Superintendent of Home Missions, presided and Reverend W.E. Day member of the Home Missions

History of Sargent County - Vol. 2 - 1880-1920 179

committee assisted. After singing, reading of scriptures and prayer, the following named all on letters of dismissal from other churches were organized into a church, which they named Milnor Presbyterian Church. Mrs. Mary M. Chandler, Mr. John Shuman, Mrs. Mary L. Shuman, Mrs. Roxanna Camfield, Mr. James H. Vail, and. Mrs. Emma F. Vail. James Vail and John Shuman were elected ruling members. James Vail, John Shuman, and F.R. Strong were elected trustees."

The church was built in 1885 at a cost of two thousand dollars and was dedicated on November 1st, 1885. Reverend Day of Lisbon preached the dedicatory sermon. The first pastor was Reverend C. W. Remington. This church was also the social center of Milnor for many years. Activities held in the church were plays, roller skating benefits, boy's socials, corn shows, flower shows and Halloween hunts. On February 1st, 1920 the church members met to burn the mortgage on the basement debt and to celebrate.

Presbyterian Ladies Group

A group of ladies met at the home of John Shuman on December 13th, 1883 to organize a ladies society. The purpose of the society was to cultivate social friendship and work "together for the advancement of Christianity by giving and doing whatsoever things are honest, whatsoever things are just and whatsoever things are of good report, to raise means to be used for building and furnishing a church." They decided to call this organization the Presbyterian Society.

"Members were Mrs. R. Camfield, it was her eighty-second birthday. Mrs. M. Chandler, Mrs. M. Young, Mrs. R. A. Burley, Mrs. Price, Mrs. Agnes Stone and Mrs. J. Bishop. Joining at the next meeting were Mrs. P. Chandler, Mrs. J. Hughes, Mrs. J. Call and Mrs. Judge Vail."

"The first Christmas program was sponsored by these ladies. It was held in the Mills Building from six to nine in the evening on Christmas day 1883." At their meetings, these ladies sewed bonnets, aprons, comforters, carpet rags, nightshirts and dolls. At their June 25th, 1885 meeting they made plans to serve a dinner in their new church on July fourth. They later held their first meeting in the new church in September 1885.

The ladies also wanted to raise money to buy a bell for the new church. To raise money they decided to build a bathhouse under the railroad water tank. The railroad company gave the cold water from the tank and the water was heated from the boilers of a pumping engine. The tank keeper's wife tended to the bath. The house and tub cost twenty-one dollars. In about one year, the ladies had purchased a bell for the steeple.

Lutheran Church

In the early days of Milnor, the Lutherans wanted to start a church. The establishment of a church started with the proposed constitution for the Milnor E. L. Church which was adopted on June 6th, 1885, "said constitution being signed by the following: Jens Zierson, E. A. Enochson, Charles Afdem and Jens Pederson, trustees and C. Louis Engh, Secretary. At a later date, the following names were added to the records: Nels O. Fordahl, Chris Jacobson, Knut Intelhouse, Albert Vaugness, Ole B. Vaugness, Andrew Grimsrude, Augustus Nelson, A. A. Fangsrude, Mrs. Carrie Nygaard, Rentsvold Frangsrude, Olaf A. Vaugness, S. A. Rundestvedt, Nels Hammenberg, Lars H. Berg, August Martinson, Peter O. Mellem, O. O. Mellem, Ole Berven, Morris Engebrigtson, Karol-ius Nelson, Hans Pederson, B. J. Engen, Jacob Anderson, Magnus Nelson, Anders Froman, Forman Carlson, Peter Skorstad, Ole Larson, Halvor Anderson, William Williams, Seavert Olson, Joe Forseth and Ole Hanson."

The congregation was served first by Reverend C. J. Selveit from 1885 to 1892. Other early ministers were:

Lutheran Church

R.A. Lavik, 1892-1913, Jacob Tanner, 1913-1916 and T. T. Roan, 1916-1919. A church building was erected in 1886 at a cost of about four thousand dollars.[34]

Milnor Lutheran Ladies Aid

"The Milnor Lutheran Ladies Aid was organized January 1st, 1886. According to the records available the following were charter members: Mrs. Cammon, Mrs. Knute Intlehouse, Mrs. Peter Intlehouse, Mrs. Neilson, Mrs. Jens Pederson, Mrs. Wicklund, Mrs. Enochson, Mrs. Vangsness, Mrs. Jacobson, Mrs. David Anderson, Mrs. Wm. Williams, and Mrs. Rheinholt Fangsrud."

"In the early days the aid met once a month in the various homes." Due to the great distance between homes, the members usually spent the entire day together. "In 1886, the Aid purchased the original church lot for thirty-five dollars. There is very little history on the early days of the Ladies Aid because no records for the aid were kept until 1935.

United Methodist Church

In May 1885, a group of Milnor residents organized a Sunday school with W.E. Patterson as superintendent. "This same group soon realized the need for a church and acted to establish the Milnor Methodist Episcopal Church on November 28th of that same year. Twenty-one members were recorded on the church rolls that year and the first minister was Reverend S.A. Danforth."[35]

In 1886, a church was built. It was a one-room structure with a wide board floor, stove, jet gaslights and chairs for seating. All social gatherings of the church were held across the street in what was known as the

Methodist Church

MCC Hall. A Ladies Aid was also organized at the same time the church was built. They held monthly meetings in various homes.³⁶

St. Arnold's Catholic Church

The first permanent Catholic Settler was Hubert Nicolai, soon joined by John Nicolai and Phillip Dietzler. A French missionary priest who lived north and west of Milnor cared for the few Catholic families. In May 1893, Father Phil Albrect of Wahpeton, made a sick call to Nicolas Nicolai. At this time he baptized John G. Nicolai, son of John and Catherine Nicolai. This is believed to be the first baptism of a white child in the area.

St. Arnold's Catholic Church

Fr. Studnicka of Hankinson held the first Catholic service December 28ᵗʰ, 1905. It was at this same time that the parish was organized. He held a few services in the old Commercial Club Hall. The first church was built in 1906 at a total cost of four thousand nine hundred seventeen dollars and seventy-nine cents. "Some of the members were: George O'Connor, Carl Winner, N.M. Stirens, Ed Sweeney, Ignatz Schonoff, Matt Wagner, Phillip Dietzler, N.J. Wolters, John Nicolai, Hubert Nicolai, and John J. O'Donnell.³⁷

On November 1ˢᵗ, 1906, Father Simon of Matador, took charge of the parish. Father Francis Meyer came from Oakes in 1912. Father Alois Jande succeeded him in 1916. "According to the marriage register, the first wedding in St. Arnold's Church was between Moses Sweeney and Anna Marie Nicolai on April 27ᵗʰ, 1908. On October 20ᵗʰ of that same year William Carpenter and Fernie Sweeney were also united in holy matrimony." A few years later on "June 6ᵗʰ, 1917 a native son, Hubert Nicolai, brought honor to the parish and community when he was ordained to the hold priesthood and

History of Sargent County - Vol. 2 - 1880-1920   183

celebrated his first Solemn High Mass in St. Arnold's Church on June 17th of that year."[38]

Milnor Organizations

The Anchor Lodge

"In the winter of 1885, a group of Milnor men organized a Masonic Lodge. The charter was issued June 10th, 1886 by the Grand Lodge of Dakota Territory and bore the name, Anchor Lodge No. 88. The leaders were: John E. Bishop, C.F. Moody, James Brown, Peter Knudson and John Morrison." Nathan Linton, David F. Vail, Philip M. Chandler, James Riddle, Albert F. Price, James Ross, Benjamin K. Rush, Lars E. Helin and Thomas Nicholson soon joined them. All charter members.[39]

"The Grand Master of Dakota Territory appointed John E. Bishop, Master; Charles F. Moody, Senior Warden and Peter Knudson, Junior Warden for opening of said lodge. After the admission of North Dakota to statehood in 1889 the charter was re-issued by authority of the Grand Lodge A. F. & A. M., of North Dakota, at its first annual communication, June 12th and 13th, 1889, as the charter of Anchor Lodge No. 25."

The Anchor Lodge met in many different locations in the early years. "The first meeting was held in the second story of the McKenzie Drug Store building." They then "moved to the second story of A. T. Fox building after its completion." Then on "February 5th, 1920, fire completely destroyed the Fox building. The building, paraphernalia and equipment were all destroyed, except records, which were kept in a fire proof safe. The lodge was again without a home. They then met temporarily in the basement of the Presbyterian Church.[40]

The Milnor Commercial Club

A Milnor Commercial Club was organized in November 1910. "The first officers elected were: President, F.W. Vail; Secretary, Roy V. Fyles; Secretary, H.K. Pennington and Treasurer, A.W. Eastman."[41]

The Smith-Thune Post No. 148

"On January 5th, 1920 a meeting of the ex-service men of World War I was held at the F.W. Vail residence, to organize a Post of the American Legion. Temporary officers were: W.H. Payne, Chairman and John Edstrom, Secretary. The following Post officers were elected: Commander, D.L. Vail; Vice Commander, Ole Tisdel; Adjutant, John Edstrom; Historian, W.H. Payne; Finance Officer, J.M. Kane; Chaplain, Reverend Edward Lee. The organization was named the Albert Smith-Lewis Thune Post No. 148 in honor and memory of two comrades in arms from Milnor and DeLamere who were killed in action in France."[42]

The Women's Temperance Union in Sargent County

Milnor had the first organized Women's Temperance Union in Sargent County. Mrs. Helen M. Barker organized the Union on March 23rd, 1887. Mrs. Barker later served as treasurer of the National W.C.T.U. with Mrs. E.D. LaSelle as president and Mrs. F.W. Runkel corresponding secretary. "Teaching the effects of alcohol and narcotics became a part of the school curriculum in 1887 and a large number of school children were members of the Loyal Temperance Legion. This union met many discouragements and some opposition, as it stood alone in the county for one year and then Rutland and Ransom were organized in 1888. Mrs. C.E. Williams, president and Mrs. A.M. Allen corresponding secretary at Rutland."

"Forman was organized in 1889 with Mrs. Emma Vail president and Miss Lida Vail corresponding secretary. Ransom in the same year with Mrs. J.R. Herring president and Mrs. J.F. Devlin corresponding secretary."

The Loyal Temperance Union at Harlem was organized in 1890 by Miss Elizabeth Preston and reorganized in 1892. A Union at Brampton was organized in 1890. Miss Preston organized the Cogswell and Vivian Unions in 1891. Miss M. Martin was president and Miss N.L. Montgomery corresponding secretary of the Cogswell Union and Mrs. S.C. Rusco president and Miss Carrie Brown corresponding secretary of Vivian. Verner was organized in 1891 with Mrs. W.E. Short president. A year later, Hamlin was organized

History of Sargent County - Vol. 2 - 1880-1920   185

with Mrs. R.C. Smith president and Mrs. Clark Wisbey corresponding secretary. A few years later in 1895 Straubville was organized with Mrs. S.M. Woolsey as president and Mrs. Cora Bush corresponding secretary.

"After the 18th Amendment to the Constitution was adopted the Unions ceased function." The Union at Milnor reorganized and disbanded several times until May 24th, 1925 when Mrs. Necie E. Buck effected the last reorganization with six members. The membership was thirty-two in September 1926.[43]

Items of Interest from *The Sargent County Teller*

November 2nd, 1883 – "The first wedding in Milnor occurred Monday afternoon at Hotel Call. Mr. Herbert Martin and Miss Sarah Crane of Ransom City were married by W.J. Hughes, Justice of the Peace."[44]

November 2nd, 1883 – "More than 25,000 bushels of wheat have been marketed in Milnor this season."

January 18th, 1884 – "The Bank of Sargent County was a new business in town. Contractors in town were now; W. Spellman, B. Johnson, P. Lewis and Engh and Co. Two butcher shops were in operation and Jens Peterson was the blacksmith. Sauder and Wolfe handled real estate."

January 18th, 1884 – "Sargent County Teller reported; "Milnor now had between three hundred and four hundred inhabitants."

February 22nd, 1884 - "Several really fine buildings have been put up. The town contains stores, saloons, hotels, lumberyards, machinery halls, a bank, doctors, lawyers, real estate dealers, wood, coal and furniture dealers, a newspaper and many other business enterprises essential to the welfare of a western town. The population of Milnor is between three and four hundred people and there are about one hundred houses. Last season the grain dealer at this place purchased about seventy-five thousand bushels of wheat, distributing about sixty thousand dollars among the farmers."

"Town lots in Milnor can be purchased very cheaply at present; the generous proprietors of the property being anxious to induce people to locate here given them all the inducements possible. The prices range from fifty dollars to four hundred dollars, according to location and demand for particulars, prices and plats. Address; Milnor Land Company or P.M. Chandler."

An Early History of Several Buildings in Milnor by Mrs. Pennington

The Jens Peterson Blacksmith shop was moved from Linton in the summer of 1883. Jens Peterson built the blacksmith shop at Barney, where he found business slack so he moved his shop to Linton and from there to Milnor when the other buildings were moved. It was located on the back of Lot 23 in Block 22 facing First Avenue. It was used as a blacksmith shop and later as an icehouse and garage.

Milnor Free Press was established in the early 1880s, owned and published by J.E. Bishop and L.V. Babcock in 1886 to 1887. Mr. William Hurly was assistant in the printing office for some time. It was owned by Ad Moore in 1889 and was not published later.

Four saloons were moved to Milnor from Linton. The number rapidly increased to eight and they outnumbered all other businesses in town. There were nine of them at one time. Milnor had two flourmills. "The first one was struck by lightning and destroyed in the early 1890s and was rebuilt and burned during the World War."[45]

The first *Free Press* office on the left, was established in the early 1880s. It was owned and published by J.E. Bishop and L.V. Babcock. It was owned by Ad Moore in 1889 and was not published after that.

Dodge Brothers Motor Cars

H.K. Pennington owned Dodge Brothers Motor Cars. This business was a dealer for Dodge Brothers Motor Cars. They may have also assembled partly finished cars. There is little information on this early business in Milnor.

Dodge Brothers Motor Cars

Dodge Brothers Work, Detroit

Jens Pederson an Early Milnor Resident

"Jens Pederson, a pioneer merchant of Milnor and one of the substantial citizens that Denmark has furnished to Sargent County, was born on the Island of Falster off the Danish coast, June 19th, 1855, a son of Peder and Marie (Rasmussen) Paulson. The father who was wagon maker by trade, died when his son Jens was but

188   *Susan Mary Kudelka*

seven years of age. Following the death of her husband Mrs. Paulson was married again, becoming the wife of Rasmus Christopherson, who came with his family to the new world in 1873 and settled in Michigan."

"Jens Pedersen did not remain there but continued on to St. Paul and soon afterward went to work in Minneapolis. He had previously learned the blacksmith's trade and he secured employment in a carriage shop in Minneapolis in which he remained for four and a half years. He then removed to Renville County, Minnesota where he embarked in business independently, opening a blacksmith shop which he carefully and successfully conducted. He also purchased one hundred and twenty-seven acres of land which he cultivated in connection with his other interests and subsequently a further purchase added one hundred and sixty acres to his holdings."

While residing on his farm, Mr. Pedersen was married in 1878 to Miss Marie Hoff, who was born in Norway, near Drammen, but came to the United States with her parents, Christian and Turina Hoff, who settled in Cottonwood County, Minnesota."

"For three years, Mr. Pedersen resided in Renville County and afterward moved to Richland County, North Dakota, in 1882, after having disposed of the interests which he had previously held. He settled three miles east of McLeod, in Richland County and as land in that locality was still in the possession of the government, he homesteaded one hundred and sixty acres, on which he built a log house. In the spring of 1883, he left that place and went to Sargent County, opening a blacksmith shop in the town of Linton, two and a half miles east of Milnor. He continued to engage in blacksmithing there until the latter part of August 1883, when he bought city lots in the new town of Milnor, which was opened up by the railroad on the 14th of August 1883. He built a shop and also a dwelling, the shop being just across the street from the site of his present store. All of the buildings in the town of Linton were then removed to Milnor but Mr. Pedersen built a home in the west part of the village, three blocks from the main street. His was the first building erected in the village and he continued to engage in blacksmithing there until 1889. In the meantime he purchased a half section of land in Milnor Township adjoining the town site and this he developed and cultivated, while engaged at the same time in blacksmithing. In 1889, he established a store for the sale of farm implements in the next block south of his blacksmith shop."[46]

Jens Pederson

The Jens Pederson Home

Birth of Milnor and Its Growth
From *The Fargo Forum and Daily Republican,* January 27th, 1916

- Following are the Boosters of Milnor and Men
Who Are Striving To Put It on the Map -

"In August 1883, the first timber was cut, the first board was sawed and the first nails were driven in the construction of buildings in the town, which has in the intervening years become the city of Milnor."

"But few of the present dwellers here have anything but the vaguest idea of what the country was or what it looked like thirty-two years ago. This lapse of time is called the life of a generation and each generation has so much to learn, so much to strive for, so many things to occupy its every thought and effort, that is gives but scant thought to the events and conditions surrounding the generation which preceded it."

"Now our thoughts are engrossed with the best service of electric light companies of telephone companies, the maintenance of proper regulations governing street traffic and of play houses, to maintaining a high standard of school and social conditions, so that only a few at times hark back to the day when the railroad pushed its iron way into the green of the virgin prairie with its invitation to the people of the cast to follow and build their homes in the new country."

"In the fall of 1882 and spring of 1883 the town at the end of the track called Linton, was a lively place and bid fair to become a good prairie town, but Severt A. Olson, the new owner of the land where it was proposed to plat the town was somewhat independent and sought to make terms with the Northern Pacific railroad which its officers thought were unreasonable. Having the power to do as they pleased they straightway exercised it –extended the line about three miles further west, laid out a goodly town site on Section 9, Township 132, Range 54 and the present city of Milnor was born. With that birth of Milnor came the death of Linton for straightway the town was moved, people and buildings to the new place. Of all those who came to the new town from the old with the recent passing away of James Brown, there remains in Milnor, but one the Hon. Jens Pederson, president of the city council and acting mayor. So quickly does the population move and shift about under the conditions under which we live. Here is also another family who can tell wonderful tales of the extinct town of Linton. John L. Tanner's living some four miles northwest of the city. Both he and his wife being among the earliest pioneers this locality can recall for the listener, the many interesting details of its building, its life and its disappearance as the buildings moving on wheels came to the town site of Milnor."

"The building up of a new country certainly makes lively towns and Milnor was no exception. The people were young and full of snap and energy. The future was full of rainbows. In a short time this lively place boasted of two hotels, many boarding houses, two newspapers, a bank, four general stores, three lumber yards, two hardware stores, two drug stores, two barber shops, a number of livery stables, three elevators, several confectionary stores, a roller skating rink and seven saloons. Having been designated the county seat for the new county of Sargent set off from Ransom county by the territorial legislature in 1884, until an election might be had by which the people of the county should themselves choose the location of the county seat, there were all the county officers and the usual accompaniment of lawyers to swell the population and contribute to

History of Sargent County - Vol. 2 - 1880-1920   191

the excitement of that period of Milnor's development. In November 1884, came the county seat election and with it a fierce contention for county offices. The result was the loss to Milnor of the county seat of Sargent County after a period of litigation."

"The people of the town being nothing daunted by this disaster, organized a normal school and maintained it for several years in the hope that it might be recognized and given permanent location when the territory became a state and the state institutions were permanently located. The loss of this normal school was the most discouraging event in the city's life. For several years matters were at the ebb, but the spirit of progressiveness, which could not long be suppressed, coupled with the natural advantages, which were behind it, Milnor came to the front once more. When fires destroyed stores and schoolhouses, better and more permanent structures took their places, trees were planted, homes built, streets grades, telephone systems –exchange and rural –joined the city to country, elevators and mills were built, burned and rebuilt, a high school system with a full four years course including domestic science and agriculture were installed and with our city streets alight with electricity by night, Milnor has come to its own –the best little city in the southern part of the state."

"The livest wires of the town can be found in The Sargent County Teller office. These are in the persons of Nels Nelson and John Edstrom. The young men looking for Milnor's interest every day with a motto of Boost for Milnor, first, last and at all times. These gentlemen took charge of The Teller the first of the past October. It is the oldest paper in the county, being established over five years ago. They are in a position to turn out the best of work, their shop being complete. They deserve the patronage of the full community."

"Few towns the size of Milnor can boast of a flour mill so complete as the one at that place. The Farmers Mill & Grain Co. is no small concern. This mill runs night and day, making an average daily of 160 barrels of flour. Most all of this being durum wheat flour which is a specialty of this mill. A small amount of this is consumed locally, the bulk of it being sent in car lots to large eastern bakeries. Elevators in connection with the mill supply the wheat. The firm is a corporation with Ole Hansen, president, Jens Pederson, vice president and C. M. Olson, secretary and treasurer."

"The Macheel Jewelry store carries a first class line of watches, clocks, jewelry, cut glass, books, stationery, camera and photo supplies. Their store is the neatest jewelry store in town and will be the largest after contemplated improvements are made. These improvements will add modern soda fountain and also a fine line of candies and cigars. This concern is handled and operated by Theo. H. Macheel, a thoroughly experienced jeweler."

"For a good homelike place to stop, The Milnor Hotel can't be excelled. J. W. Robinson, proprietor, has a way of making one feel thoroughly at home. He gives the best of attention to the commercial trade and serves meals that are a pleasure to sit down to. Steam heated rooms with bath privileges adds to the comfort of his hostelry. Mr. Robinson has had charge of this hotel since November only in which time he has made extensive improvements as to repairing and cleaning. He comes from Minneapolis, formerly being a road man."

"The First National bank has a capital and surplus of $30,000 a strong bank having the full confidence of the entire community. The officers of the institution are: E. B. Johnson, president, Peter Christiansen, vice president, A. W. Eastman, cashier and Otto Miller, assistant cashier. A picture of their building is shown in this issue."

"In the line of real estate firms, Doyle Bros., are the leaders. They handle fine improved farms in Sargent, Richland and Ransom counties. Farms on which 106 bushels of corn have been known to grow per single acre. These lands are of the best. F. M. Doyle is also owner of the hotel. This building is for sale by him at the present time."

History of Sargent County - Vol. 2 - 1880-1920   193

"Milnor may consider herself fortunate in having an up to date hardware store. A store that carries as complete a line, as does the Milnor Hardware Co. is a credit to any community. This corporation is owned and controlled by local men with Hans Johnson as acting president and treasurer and J. K. Taylor, vice president."

"For a well equipped pharmacy, Milnor is not outclassed. S. C. Hoel manager and owner of the drug store is in a position to give his patrons the best of service and anything that is desired in his line. His drug, medicine and toilet article stock is complete, carrying further a supply of kodaks, cut glass, china and other articles that are found in a first class pharmacy."

"For city dray service, H. K. Brown delivers the goods. General draying, baggage transfers and freight work are his specialties. At any time you will be able to find H. K. around and always ready to lend his help."

"In this issue will be seen a cut of Farmers Grain & Trading Co. This is strictly a farmer's organization, organized for the purpose of conducting a farmer's elevator. This has been very successful handling since June 1st, 225,000 bushels of grain. Their building is new and modern. The officers of this concern are as follows: William Busching, president, Pete Christianson, vice president, A. A. Stockstad, secretary, D. A. Cross, treasurer and H. E. Wyum, manager. Other directors, E. C. Enge, H. P. Holt, Wm. Sebens and C. W. Warner."

"When you want to see a good farm, don't forget that of A. Fadness or J. O. Nordstrom. Both are complete and will give you a good impression of what can be done with North Dakota lands. Diversified farming is strong in both places, stock raising, in connection with the culture of the grain being prominent."

194   *Susan Mary Kudelka*

[1] An Early History of Milnor and Milnor Township, *Milnor's 75th Anniversary Community Book 1883-1958.*

[2] The Galloping Goose, *100 Years of Milnor Memories 1883-1983*, (Gwinner, J & M Printing, 1983), 8.

[3] Railroad, *The Teller Centennial Edition* pg. B36.

[4] Galloping Goose, 100 Years of Milnor Memories, 8.

[5] Railroad History, 100 Years of Milnor Memories, 11.

[6] Railroad, The Teller Centennial Edition, B36.

[7] Railroad History, 100 Years of Milnor Memories, 11-12.

[8] Railroad, The Teller Centennial Edition, B36.

[9] Milnor's Early Business and Professional Men, *Milnor's 75th book,* 17-18.

[10] Milnor's Past Business and Professional People, 100 Years of Milnor Memories, 36-37.

[11] Milnor's City Government, Milnor's 75th book, 20.

[12] Milnor's City Government, 100 Years of Milnor Memories, 12.

[13] An Early History of Milnor and Milnor Township, *Milnor's 75th book,* 12-14.

[14] The Milnor Post Office Established in October 1883, Milnor's 75th book, 71.

[15] An Early History of Milnor, *Milnor's 75th book,* 14.

[16] An Early History of Milnor, *Milnor's 75th book,* 14.

[17] History of the Milnor Fire Department, 100 Years of Milnor Memories, 67-68.

[18] Milnor Rural Telephone, 100 Years of Milnor Memories, 39.

[19] Farmers Grain & Trading Company, 100 Years of Milnor Memories, 48.

[20] Past Businesses of Milnor, Thompson Yards, 100 Years of Milnor Memories, 39.

[21] Milnor Clothing and Dianne's Country Charm, 100 Years of Milnor Memories, 51.

[22] Past Businesses of Milnor, Co-operative Creamery, 100 Years of Milnor Memories, 38-39.

[23] Milnor Theatre, 100 Years of Milnor Memories, 52.

[24] Edison Motors, 100 Years of Milnor Memories, 47-48.

[25] History of Milnor, 100 Years of Milnor Memories, 1.

[26] Early History of Banking in Sargent County, Milnor's 75th book, 23.

[27] History of the First National Bank, 100 Years of Milnor Memories, 49.

[28] Early History of Banking in Sargent County, Milnor's 75th book, 23.

[29] Milnor's Schools Have Grown with Our Community, Milnor's 75th book, 21-22.

[30] Milnor's Schools Have Grown with Our Community, Milnor's 75th book, 21-22.

[31] From Milnor's 75th book, 21-22 and from the History of Sargent County and Milnor Township.

[32] Milnor's Schools Have Grown with Our Community, Milnor's 75th book, 21-22.

[33] History of Sargent County and Milnor Township a communication written by A. M. Simpson former county superintendent of schools by Mary Wolfe Pennington, 1926.

[34] History of the Lutheran Church, Milnor 75th book, 47-48.

[35] United Methodist Church, 100 Years of Milnor Memories, 59.

[36] Milnor Methodist Church History, Milnor's 75th book, 46.

[37] St. Arnold's Catholic Church, 100 Years of Milnor Memories, 57.

[38] St. Arnold's, Milnor's 75th book, 41.

[39] History of Anchor Lodge, 100 Years of Milnor Memories, 64.

[40] History of Anchor Lodge, Milnor's 75th book, 27.

[41] Milnor Merchant's Club, 100 Years of Milnor Memories, 69.

[42] History of Smith-Thune Post No. 148, 100 Years of Milnor Memories, 72.

[43] The Women's Temperance Union in Sargent County, from the History of Sargent County and Milnor Township, Pennington, book 2.

[44] Excerpt from the Teller, 100 Years of Milnor Memories, 59.

[45] History of Sargent County and Milnor Township, Pennington.

[46] Jens Pedersen, 100 Years of Milnor Memories, 43.

Milnor in the 1880s.

A Milnor cycle club about 1898.

Christianson's Store

Bottom: Inside Arnold Christianson's Drug Store, the men are from left to right, Will Kern, he worked in the bank, Bud Allen, he did odd jobs, Harry Brown, drayman and J.K. Taylor, from the lumberyard. The photo was taken around 1900.

Park's Livery Stable, 1905-1910.

Milnor in the early 1900s.

Main Street in the early days.

The Milnor Lumber Company started about 1900 with J.K. Taylor as manager.

A Milnor post card in the summer of 1910.

Milnor bird's eye view.

Milnor Depot in 1911.

The divide on Storm Lake.

Waiting for the train at the Milnor Depot.

The Farmers Mill and Grain Company.

J. A. WALSH,
ATTORNEY AT LAW,
Real : Estate, : Loan : and : Insurance : Agent.

COLLECTIONS, CONTESTS, AND FINAL PROOFS A SPECIALTY.

Real Estate Bought and Sold.——Taxes Paid for Non-Residents.

LINTON, SARGENT CO., D. T.
Direct Letters via Wahpeton, D. T.)

J.A. Walsh an attorney at Linton.

In the center is Sargent County's first courthouse at Milnor. To the left is the *Sargent County Teller* office.

The Jorgenson, Nelson and Austin Store.

An early Milnor hotel.

An early Milnor restaurant.

Flatens Store

Inside Sherdan's Bar, pictured are Clayton Stockstad, Lars Hague, Bob Weeks, Levi Shoemaker, Chas. Boatman, Warnie Edwards and Hans Johnson.

Men from the Milnor Woodmen's Lodge.

Mill fire on September 23rd, 1917 at 5:10 am. The photo was taken by Anderson Studio.

A Milnor High School Glee Club in 1917.

A Milnor football team in 1920.

Dad White, a Milnor Policeman during the 1920s.

Main Street in 1918.

Main Street in 1920.

Susan Mary Kudelka

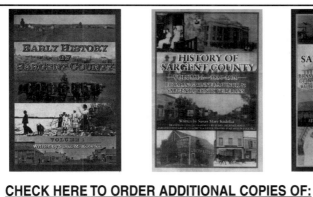

CHECK HERE TO ORDER ADDITIONAL COPIES OF:
- ❏ **EARLY HISTORY OF SARGENT COUNTY - _VOLUME 1_**
- ❏ **HISTORY OF SARGENT COUNTY - _VOLUME 2_ 1880-1920**
  (Forman, Gwinner, Milnor & Sargent County Veterans
- ❏ **HISTORY OF SARGENT COUNTY - _VOLUME 3_ 1880-1920**
  (Brampton, Cayuga, Cogswell, Crete, DeLamere, Geneseo, Harlem, Havana, Rutland, Stirum & Other History)

$16.95 EACH
(plus $3.95 shipping & handling for first book,
add $2.00 for each additional book ordered.
Shipping and Handling costs for larger quantites available upon request.

Please send me
_____ VOLUME 1   _____ VOLUME 2   _____ VOLUME 3
additional books at $16.95 + shipping & handling

Bill my: ❏ VISA   ❏ MasterCard   Expires _____
Card # _____
Signature _____
Daytime Phone Number _____

For credit card orders call 1-888-568-6329
TO ORDER ON-LINE VISIT: www.jmcompanies.com
OR SEND THIS ORDER FORM TO:
McCleery & Sons Publishing• PO Box 248 • Gwinner, ND 58040-0248
I am enclosing $_____   ❏ Check ❏ Money Order
Payable in US funds. No cash accepted.

SHIP TO:
Name _____
Mailing Address _____
City _____
State/Zip _____

Orders by check allow longer delivery time. Money order and credit card orders will be shipped within 48 hours. This offer is subject to change without notice.

a division of J&M Companies

Call 1-888-568-6329
to order by credit card OR order
on-line at www.jmcompanies.com

NEW RELEASES

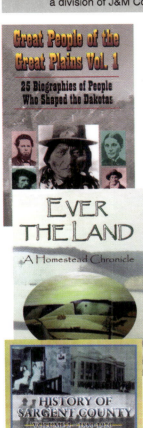

Great People of the Great Plains Vol. 1
25 Biographies of People Who Shaped the Dakotas
This is the second book for Keith Norman and the first in this series. Keith has always had an interest in the history of the region. His radio show 'Great Stories of the Great Plains' is heard on great radio stations all across both Dakotas. While the biographies within this book are a bit too long to fit the time constraints of a radio show, listeners will find the events and people portrayed familiar. For more information on the radio show and a list of his current affiliates check out Norman's website at www.tumbleweednetwork.com.
Written by Keith Norman - Author of *Great Stories of the Great Plains - Tales of the Dakotas* (124 pgs.)
$14.95 each in a 6x9" paperback.

Ever The Land
A Homestead Chronicle
This historical chronicle (non-fiction) traces the life of young Pehr through his youth in the 1800's, marriage, parenthood and tenant farming in Sweden; then his emigration to America and homesteading in Minnesota. Multifarious simple joys and woes, and one deep constant sorrow accompany Pehr to his grave in 1914.
Written by: The late Ruben L. Parson (336 pgs.)
$16.96 each in a 6x9" paperback.

History of Sargent County - Volume 2 - 1880-1920
(Forman, Gwinner, Milnor & Sargent County Veterans)
Over 220 photos and seven chapters containing: Forman, Gwinner and Milnor, North Dakota history with surveyed maps from 1909. Plus Early History of Sargent County, World War I Veterans, Civil War Veterans and Sargent County Fair History.
Written by: Susan Mary Kudelka - Author of *Early History of Sargent County - Volume 1* (224 pgs.)
$16.95 each in a 6x9" paperback.

History of Sargent County - Volume 3 - 1880-1920
(Brampton, Cayuga, Cogswell, Crete, DeLamere, Geneseo, Harlem, Havana, Rutland, Stirum & Other History)
Over 280 photos and fifteen chapters containing: Brampton, Cayuga, Cogswell, Crete, DeLamere, Geneseo, Harlem, Havana, Rutland and Stirum, North Dakota histories with surveyed maps from 1909. Plus history on Sargent County in WWI, Sargent County Newspapers, E. Hamilton Lee and bonus photo section.
Written by: Susan Mary Kudelka - Author of *Early History of Sargent County - Volume 1* (220 pgs.)
$16.95 each in a 6x9" paperback.

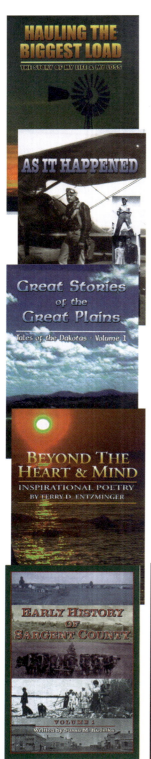

Hauling the Biggest Load - *The Story of My Life & My Loss*
This is an unusual story because of the many changes that have happened since the author's birth in 1926. In May 2002, he lost his son, John, in a car accident. None of those other experiences seemed important anymore... Richard needed something to try and take his mind off that tragedy. "I thought I had hauled some big loads in my life but I never had to have a load as big as this one."
Written by: Richard Hamann (144 pages)
$14.95 each in 6x9" paperback.

As It Happened
Over 40 photos and several chapters containing Allen Saunders' early years, tales of riding the rails, his Navy career, marriage, Army instruction, flying over "The Hump", and his return back to North Dakota.
Written by Allen E. Saunders. (74 pgs)
$12.95 each in a 6x9" paperback.

Great Stories of the Great Plains - *Tales of the Dakotas - Vol. 1*
The radio show "Great Stories of the Great Plains" is heard on great radio stations all across both Dakotas. Norman has taken some of the stories from broadcasts, added some details, and even added some complete new tales to bring together this book of North and South Dakota history.
Written by Keith Norman. (134 pgs.)
$14.95 each in a 6x9" paperback.

Beyond the Heart & Mind
Inspirational Poetry by Terry D. Entzminger
Beyond the Heart & Mind is the first in a series of inspirational poetry collections of Entzminger. Read and cherish over 100 original poems and true-to-the-heart verses printed in full color in the following sections: Words of Encouragement, On the Wings of Prayer, God Made You Very Special, Feelings From Within, The True Meaning of Love, and Daily Joys. (120 pgs.)
$12.95 each in a 6x9" paperback.

Early History of Sargent County - *Volume 1*
Over seventy photos and thirty-five chapters containing the early history of Sargent County, North Dakota: Glacial Movement in Sargent County, Native Americans in Sargent County, Weather, Memories of the Summer of 1883, Fight for the County Seat, Townships, Surveyed Maps from 1882 and much more.
Written by Susan M. Kudelka. (270 pgs.)
$16.95 each in a 6x9" paperback.

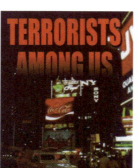

Terrorists Among Us
This piece of fiction was written to "expose a weakness" in present policies and conflicts in the masses of rules which seem to put emphasis on business, money, and power interests at the expense of the people's security, safety and happiness. Shouldn't we and our leaders strive for some security for our people?
Written by Carl Aabye & R.J. Letnes. (178 pgs.)
$15.95 each in a 6x9" paperback.

THE HASTINGS SERIES

Blue Darkness *(First in a Series of Hastings Books)*
This tale of warm relationships and chilling murders takes place in the lake country of central Minnesota. Normal activities in the small town of New Dresen are disrupted when local resident, ex-CIA agent Maynard Cushing, is murdered. His killer, Robert Ranforth also an ex-CIA agent, had been living anonymously in the community for several years. to the anonymous ex-agent. Stalked and attached at his country home, he employs tools and people to mount a defense and help solve crimes. Written by Ernest Francis Schanilec (author of The Towers). (276 pgs.) $16.95 each in a 6x9" paperback.

The Towers *(Second in a Series of Hastings Books)*
Tom Hastings has moved from the lake country of central Minnesota to Minneapolis. His move was precipitated by the trauma associated with the murder of one of his neighbors. After renting an apartment on the 20th floor of a high-rise apartment building known as The Towers, he's met new friends and retained his relationship with a close friend, Julie, from St. Paul. Hastings is a resident of the high-rise for less than a year when a young lady is found murdered next to a railroad track, a couple of blocks from The Towers. The murderer shares the same elevators, lower-level garage and other areas in the high-rise as does Hastings. The building manager and other residents, along with Hastings are caught up in dramatic events that build to a crisis while the local police are baffled. Who is the killer? Written by Ernest Francis Schanilec. (268 pgs.) $16.95 each in a 6x9" paperback.

Danger In The Keys *(Third in a Series of Hastings Books)*
Tom Hastings is looking forward to a month's vacation in Florida. While driving through Tennessee, he witnesses an automobile leaving the road and plunging down a steep slope. He stops and assists another man in finding the car. The driver, a young woman, survives the accident. Tom is totally unaware that the young woman was being chased because she had chanced coming into possession of a valuable gem, which had been heisted from a Saudi Arabian prince in a New York hotel room. After arriving in Key Marie Island in Florida, Tom checks in and begins enjoying the surf and the beach. He meets many interesting people, however, some of them are on the island because of the Guni gem, and they will stop at nothing in order to gain possession. Desperate people and their greedy ambitions interrupt Tom's goal of a peaceful vacation. Written by Ernest Francis Schanilec (210 pgs.)
$16.95 each in a 6x9" paperback.

Purgatory Curve *(Fourth in a Series of Hastings Books)*
A loud horn penetrated the silence on a September morning in New Dresden, Minnesota. Tom Hastings stepped onto Main Street sidewalk after emerging from the corner Hardware Store. He heard a freight train coming and watched in horror as it crushed a pickup truck that was stalled on the railroad tracks. Moments before the crash, he saw someone jump from the cab. An elderly farmer's body was later recovered from the mangled vehicle. Tom was interviewed by the sheriff the next day and was upset that his story about what he saw wasn't believed. The tragic death of the farmer was surrounded with controversy and mysterious people, including a nephew who taunted Tom after the accident. Or, was it an accident?   Written by Ernest Francis Schanilec (210 pgs.) $16.95 each in a 6x9" paperback.

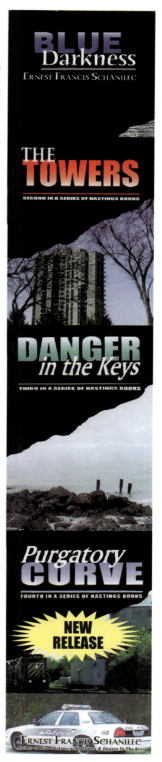

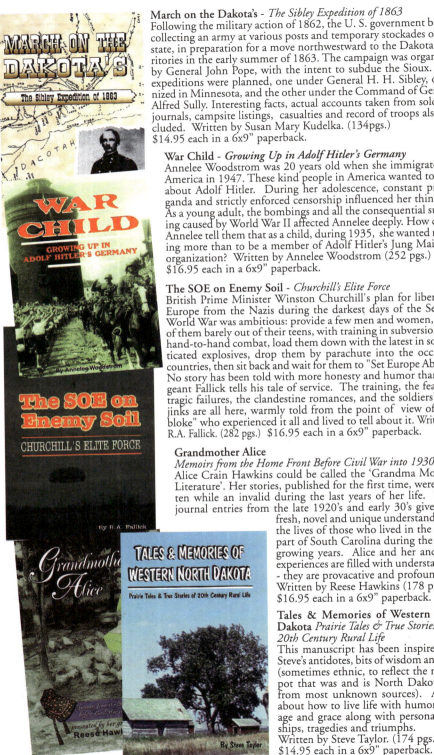

March on the Dakota's - *The Sibley Expedition of 1863*
Following the military action of 1862, the U. S. government began collecting an army at various posts and temporary stockades of the state, in preparation for a move northwestward to the Dakota Territories in the early summer of 1863. The campaign was organized by General John Pope, with the intent to subdue the Sioux. Two expeditions were planned, one under General H. H. Sibley, organized in Minnesota, and the other under the Command of General Alfred Sully. Interesting facts, actual accounts taken from soldiers' journals, campsite listings, casualties and record of troops also included. Written by Susan Mary Kudelka. (134pgs.)
$14.95 each in a 6x9" paperback.

War Child - *Growing Up in Adolf Hitler's Germany*
Annelee Woodstrom was 20 years old when she immigrated to America in 1947. These kind people in America wanted to hear about Adolf Hitler. During her adolescence, constant propaganda and strictly enforced censorship influenced her thinking. As a young adult, the bombings and all the consequential suffering caused by World War II affected Annelee deeply. How could Annelee tell them that as a child, during 1935, she wanted nothing more than to be a member of Adolf Hitler's Jung Maidens' organization? Written by Annelee Woodstrom (252 pgs.)
$16.95 each in a 6x9" paperback.

The SOE on Enemy Soil - *Churchill's Elite Force*
British Prime Minister Winston Churchill's plan for liberating Europe from the Nazis during the darkest days of the Second World War was ambitious: provide a few men and women, most of them barely out of their teens, with training in subversion and hand-to-hand combat, load them down with the latest in sophisticated explosives, drop them by parachute into the occupied countries, then sit back and wait for them to "Set Europe Ablaze." No story has been told with more honesty and humor than Sergeant Fallick tells his tale of service. The training, the fear, the tragic failures, the clandestine romances, and the soldiers' high jinks are all here, warmly told from the point of view of "one bloke" who experienced it all and lived to tell about it. Written by R.A. Fallick. (282 pgs.) $16.95 each in a 6x9" paperback.

Grandmother Alice
Memoirs from the Home Front Before Civil War into 1930's
Alice Crain Hawkins could be called the 'Grandma Moses of Literature'. Her stories, published for the first time, were written while an invalid during the last years of her life. These journal entries from the late 1920's and early 30's gives us a fresh, novel and unique understanding of the lives of those who lived in the upper part of South Carolina during the state's growing years. Alice and her ancestors experiences are filled with understanding - they are provacative and profound. Written by Reese Hawkins (178 pgs.)
$16.95 each in a 6x9" paperback.

Tales & Memories of Western North Dakota *Prairie Tales & True Stories of 20th Century Rural Life*
This manuscript has been inspired with Steve's antidotes, bits of wisdom and jokes (sometimes ethnic, to reflect the melting pot that was and is North Dakota; and from most unknown sources). A story about how to live life with humor, courage and grace along with personal hardships, tragedies and triumphs.
Written by Steve Taylor. (174 pgs.)
$14.95 each in a 6x9" paperback.

Phil Lempert's HEALTHY, WEALTHY, & WISE
The Shoppers Guide for Today's Supermarket
This is the must-have tool for getting the most for your money in every aisle. With this valuable advice you will never see (or shop) the supermarket the same way again. You will learn how to: save at least $1,000 a year on your groceries, guarantee satisfaction on every shopping trip, get the most out of coupons or rebates, avoid marketing gimmicks, create the ultimate shopping list, read and understand the new food labels, choose the best supermarkets for you and your family. Written by Phil Lempert. (198 pgs.)
$9.95 each in a 6x9" paperback.

Miracles of COURAGE
The Larry W. Marsh Story
This story is for anyone looking for simple formulas for overcoming insurmountable obstacles. At age 18, Larry lost both legs in a traffic accident and learned to walk again on untested prosthesis. No obstacle was too big for him - putting himself through college - to teaching a group of children that frustrated the whole educational system - to developing a nationally recognized educational program to help these children succeed. Written by Linda Marsh. (134 pgs.)
$12.95 each in a 6x9" paperback.

The Garlic Cure
Learn about natural breakthroughs to outwit: Allergies, Arthritis, Cancer, Candida Albicans, Colds, Flu and Sore Throat, Environmental and Body Toxins, Fatigue, High Cholesterol, High Blood Pressure and Homocysteine and Sinus Headaches. The most comprehensive, factual and brightly written health book on garlic of all times. INCLUDES: 139 GOURMET GARLIC RECIPES! Written by James F. Scheer, Lynn Allison and Charlie Fox. (240 pgs.)
$14.95 each in a 6x9" paperback.

I Took The Easy Way Out
Life Lessons on Hidden Handicaps
Twenty-five years ago, Tom Day was managing a growing business - holding his own on the golf course and tennis court. He was living in the fast lane. For the past 25 years, Tom has spent his days in a wheelchair with a spinal cord injury. Attendants serve his every need. What happened to Tom? We get an honest account of the choices Tom made in his life. It's a courageous story of reckoning, redemption and peace. Written by Thomas J. Day. (200 pgs.)
$19.95 each in a 6x9" paperback.

9/11 and Meditation - *America's Handbook*
All Americans have been deeply affected by the terrorist events of and following 9-11-01 in our country. David Thorson submits that meditation is a potentially powerful intervention to ameliorate the frightening effects of such divisive and devastating acts of terror. This book features a lifetime of harrowing life events amidst intense pychological and social polarization, calamity and chaos; overcome in part by practicing the age-old art of meditation. Written by David Thorson. (110 pgs.)
$9.95 each in a 4-1/8 x 7-1/4" paperback.

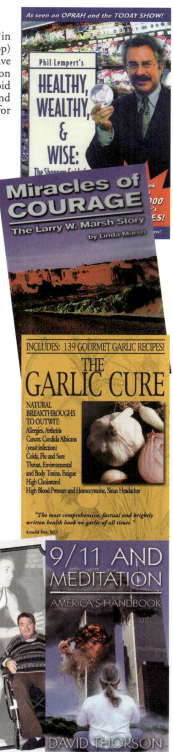

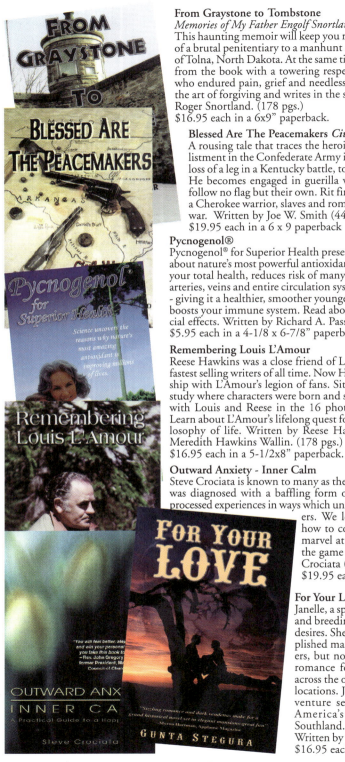

From Graystone to Tombstone
Memories of My Father Engolf Snortland 1908-1976
This haunting memoir will keep you riveted with true accounts of a brutal penitentiary to a manhunt in the unlikely little town of Tolna, North Dakota. At the same time the reader will emerge from the book with a towering respect for the author, a man who endured pain, grief and needless guilt -- but who learned the art of forgiving and writes in the spirit of hope. Written by Roger Snortland. (178 pgs.)
$16.95 each in a 6x9" paperback.

Blessed Are The Peacemakers *Civil War in the Ozarks*
A rousing tale that traces the heroic Rit Gatlin from his enlistment in the Confederate Army in Little Rock to his tragic loss of a leg in a Kentucky battle, to his return in the Ozarks. He becomes engaged in guerilla warfare with raiders who follow no flag but their own. Rit finds himself involved with a Cherokee warrior, slaves and romance in a land ravaged by war. Written by Joe W. Smith (444 pgs.)
$19.95 each in a 6 x 9 paperback

Pycnogenol®
Pycnogenol® for Superior Health presents exciting new evidence about nature's most powerful antioxidant. Pycnogenol® improves your total health, reduces risk of many diseases, safeguards your arteries, veins and entire circulation system. It protects your skin - giving it a healthier, smoother younger glow. Pycnogenol® also boosts your immune system. Read about it's many other beneficial effects. Written by Richard A. Passwater, Ph.D. (122 pgs.)
$5.95 each in a 4-1/8 x 6-7/8" paperback.

Remembering Louis L'Amour
Reese Hawkins was a close friend of Louis L'Amour, one of the fastest selling writers of all time. Now Hawkins shares this friendship with L'Amour's legion of fans. Sit with Reese in L'Amour's study where characters were born and stories came to life. Travel with Louis and Reese in the 16 photo pages in this memoir. Learn about L'Amour's lifelong quest for knowledge and his philosophy of life. Written by Reese Hawkins and his daughter Meredith Hawkins Wallin. (178 pgs.)
$16.95 each in a 5-1/2x8" paperback.

Outward Anxiety - Inner Calm
Steve Crociata is known to many as the Optician to the Stars. He was diagnosed with a baffling form of cancer. The author has processed experiences in ways which uniquely benefit today's readers. We learn valuable lessons on how to cope with distress, how to marvel at God, and how to win at the game of life. Written by Steve Crociata (334 pgs.)
$19.95 each in a 6 x 9 paperback

For Your Love
Janelle, a spoiled socialite, has beauty and breeding to attract any mate she desires. She falls for Jared, an accomplished man who has had many lovers, but no real love. Their hesitant romance follows Jared and Janelle across the ocean to exciting and wild locations. Join in a romance and adventure set in the mid-1800's in America's grand and proud Southland.
Written by Gunta Stegura. (358 pgs.)
$16.95 each in a 6x9" paperback.

Bonanza Belle
In 1908, Carrie Amundson left her home to become employed on a bonanza farm. Carrie married and moved to town. One tragedy after the other befell her and altered her life considerably and she found herself back on the farm where her family lived the toiled during the Great Depression. Carrie was witness to many life-changing events happenings. She changed from a carefree girl to a woman of great depth and stamina.
Written by Elaine Ulness Swenson. (344 pgs.)
$15.95 each in a 6x8-1/4" paperback.

Home Front
Read the continuing story of Carrie Amundson, whose life in North Dakota began in *Bonanza Belle*. This is the story of her family, faced with the challenges, sacrifices and hardships of World War II. Everything changed after the Pearl Harbor attack, and ordinary folk all across America, on the home front, pitched in to help in the war effort. Even years after the war's end, the effects of it are still evident in many of the men and women who were called to serve their country.
Written by Elaine Ulness Swenson. (304 pgs.)
$15.95 each in a 6x8-1/4" paperback.

First The Dream
This story spans ninety years of Anna's life - from Norway to America - to finding love and losing love. She and her family experience two world wars, flu epidemics, the Great Depression, droughts and other quirks of Mother Nature and the Vietnam War. A secret that Anna has kept is fully revealed at the end of her life. Written by Elaine Ulness Swenson. (326 pgs.)
$15.95 each in a 6x8-1/4" paperback

Pay Dirt
An absorbing story reveals how a man with the courage to follow his dream found both gold and unexpected adventure and adversity in Interior Alaska, while learning that human nature can be the most unpredictable of all.
Written by Otis Hahn & Alice Vollmar. (168 pgs.)
$15.95 each in a 6x9" paperback.

Spirits of Canyon Creek *Sequel to "Pay Dirt"*
Hahn has a rich stash of true stories about his gold mining experiences. This is a continued successful collaboration of battles on floodwaters, facing bears and the discovery of gold in the Yukon. Written by Otis Hahn & Alice Vollmar. (138 pgs.)
$15.95 each in a 6x9" paperback.

Seasons With Our Lord
Original seasonal and special event poems written from the heart. Feel the mood with the tranquil color photos facing each poem. A great coffee table book or gift idea. Written by Cheryl Lebahn Hegvik. (68 pgs.)
$24.95 each in a 11x8-1/2 paperback.

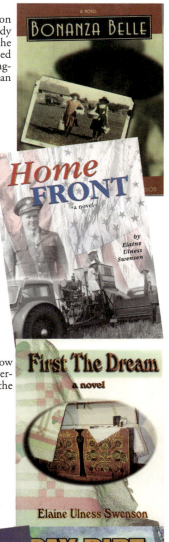

Damsel in a Dress
Escape into a world of reflection and after thought with this second printing of Larson's first poetry book. It is her intention to connect people with feelings and touch the souls of people who have experienced similiar times. Lynne emphasizes the belief that everything happens for a reason. After all, with every event in life come lessons...we grow from hardships. It gives us character and it made her who she is. Written by Lynne D. Richard Larson (author of Eat, Drink & Remarry) (86 pgs.)
$12.95 each in a 5x8" paperback.

Eat, Drink & Remarry
The poetry in this book is taken from different experiences in Lynne's life and from different geographical and different emotional places. Every poem is an inspiration from someone or a direct event from their life...or from hers. Every victory and every mistake - young or old. They slowly shape and mold you into the unique person you are. Celebrate them as rough times that you were strong enough to endure. Written by Lynne D. Richard Larson (86 pgs.) $12.95 each in a 5x8" paperback.

Country-fied
Stories with a sense of humor and love for country and small town people who, like the author, grew up country-fied . . . Country-fied people grow up with a unique awareness of their dependence on the land. They live their lives with dignity, hard work, determination and the ability to laugh at themselves.
Written by Elaine Babcock. (184 pgs.)
$14.95 each in a 6x9" paperback.

Charlie's Gold and Other Frontier Tales
Kamron's first collection of short stories gives you adventure tales about men and women of the west, made up of cowboys, Indians, and settlers. Written by Kent Kamron.
(174 pgs.) $15.95 each in a 6x9" paperback.

A Time For Justice
This second collection of Kamron's short stories takes off where the first volume left off, satisfying the reader's hunger for more tales of the wide prairie. Written by Kent Kamron. (182 pgs.) $16.95 each in a 6x9" paperback.

It Really Happened Here!
Relive the days of farm-to-farm salesmen and hucksters, of ghost ships and locust plagues when you read Ethelyn Pearson's collection of strange but true tales. It captures the spirit of our ancestors in short, easy to read, colorful accounts that will have you yearning for more. Written by Ethelyn Pearson. (168 pgs.) $24.95 each in an 8-1/2x11" paperback.

The Silk Robe
Dedicated to Shari Lynn Hunt, a wonderful woman who passed away from cancer. Mom lived her life with unfailing faith, an open loving heart and a giving spirit. She is remembered for her compassion and gentle strength. Written by Shaunna Privratsky.
$6.95 each in a 4-1/4x5-1/2" booklet. *Complimentary notecard and envelope included.*

(Add $3.95 shipping & handling for first book, add $2.00 for each additional book ordered.)